Multimedia in Higher Education

A Practical Guide to New Tools for Interactive Teaching and Learning

Multimedia in Higher Education

A Practical Guide to New Tools for Interactive Teaching and Learning

Dennis R. Falk
and
Helen L. Carlson

University of Minnesota, Duluth

Learned Information, Inc.
Medford, NJ
1995

Contents

Foreword

This book was developed in response to the emerging technologies that provide unlimited potential for interactive teaching and learning; yet, these technologies are little used in higher education. Multimedia is a relatively new development, and many faculty members find it difficult to gain the knowledge required to use its resources effectively.

The authors have engaged in numerous applications of multimedia instruction in higher education: they have developed original interactive videodiscs; repurposed already developed materials; and used new multimedia applications in our classes. They have systemically studied various aspects of instruction. These include the use of large group, small group, and individualized instruction; the use of inductive and deductive instructional designs; and the match of learning styles to instruction offered. Through theoretical study, research experimentation, and practical application, the authors have gained knowledge that they would like to share with other faculty members in higher education.

The book is designed to offer an overall paradigm for design of instruction related to multimedia, and to explore each step of the paradigm with reviews of the literature, lists of pertinent questions, case studies, guidelines, and resource suggestions. While items in the literature reviews may suggest some overarching theoretical issues, the authors' primary focus remains on offering a practical guide to professors in higher education: those who are just beginning to think about using multimedia as well as those who already use that technology in their classrooms and learning laboratories. Because the technology underlying multimedia hardware and software is expanding rapidly, this book should be used as a starting point for further study.

The authors wish to acknowledge the base of learning about multimedia that was developed in their interactions with members of the Videodisc Research Group at the University of Minnesota, Duluth. These people include John Keener, Iver Bogen, Eugene Grossman, Mark Nierengarten, Harry Watts, Alvin Ollenburger, and Vern Simula of the University of Minnesota, Duluth, and Larry K. Bright, who is now Dean of Education at the University of South Dakota. They also wish to thank the numerous experts in subject matter and instructional design who contributed to their deepened understanding of the use of multimedia. Finally, they also wish to acknowledge the input of their students who graciously consented to participate in numerous formative and summative evaluation studies and who offered their insights about improving instruction through the use of multimedia.

PART 1

Introduction, Process, and Problem

Part 1 provides a foundation for understanding how multimedia can become an effective teaching and learning tool in higher education. Before examining the nature of the hardware and applications of multimedia, we present and explain a general problem solving process. In addition, Part 1 explores the general nature of educational problems that higher education faces today.

Chapter 1 introduces several aspects of multimedia. An overview of the current state of multimedia tools is followed by three scenarios describing different uses of multimedia as a teaching and learning tool. Lack of knowledge about multimedia is identified as a key limiting factor preventing its wider use in higher education, and we describe the format this book follows to provide the necessary knowledge.

Chapter 2 looks at a problem solving approach to the development and use of multimedia in higher education. Instructional design activities are described and integrated into a problem solving format that consists of (1) defining the higher education problem to be addressed, (2) generating a variety of multimedia and other instructional solutions, (3) selecting the solutions to be adopted, (4) implementing the multimedia solutions, and (5) evaluating whether instructional solutions incorporating multimedia have effectively addressed the defined problem. Questions and guidelines related to this problem solving approach, and an example using instructional design activities within that approach are provided.

Chapter 3 defines the general problems and opportunities now present in higher education. The general nature of the higher education setting, the changing characteristics of students in higher education, and the broad goals of higher education are reviewed. Questions related to these issues are posed, examples are offered, and guidelines and resources for further explorations are provided.

CHAPTER 1

INTRODUCTION

Interactive multimedia identifies a relatively new technology that integrates a variety of media—including video, sound, music, photographs, drawings, computer graphics, and animation—in a single electronic medium, and it provides the ability to link ideas in a nonlinear format. As a rapidly developing technology, innovations in both hardware and software appear continuously, so that an enduring definition of multimedia remains elusive. Even the name for the technology is in flux—some would prefer *hypermedia*. In this book, the term *interactive multimedia* refers to educational technologies that allow for nonlinear linking of a variety of media forms.

Multimedia in its most established form combines the advantages of computer-assisted instruction with those of interactive videodiscs, and generally is referred to as *interactive video*. The videodisc portion of this system can store and provide very rapid random access to 54,000 video images and sixty minutes of high-quality audio. The computer controls which video images and audio are displayed on the color monitor. Computer text, digitized video and sound, animation, and sophisticated graphics can be added to the monitor screen. Thus, any instruction that a computer or videotapes can provide, or any synergistic combination of the two, can be incorporated into multimedia applications.

The options for multimedia systems have recently expanded beyond videodiscs (Galbreath, 1992a). For most of the 1980s, multimedia (as defined in this book) was delivered by a computer-controlled videodisc, which contained analog-recorded data. Increasingly, with the rapid advances in digital and computer technology, it is the digital-based storage platforms (multimedia hardware systems) that are gaining attention for multimedia delivery. Compact disc read-only memory (CD-ROM), digital video interactive (DVI), compact disc-interactive (CD-I), and other digital-based platforms are evolving rapidly, and on the horizon loom new technologies that will further enhance the capabilities of multimedia.

One can best get a sense of interactive multimedia power by using the technology first hand—and we encourage readers to do so at every opportunity. If you have not yet had first-hand experience, the following scenarios will provide a flavor of what is possible.

3

Scenario Number One

Professor Susan Ross stands in a medium-sized auditorium classroom before 150 freshman and sophomore students in an introductory biology class. The topic for today's class is cell reproduction, and the students are watching a 10-foot by 15-foot screen at the front of the room. Professor Ross defines the concept of *mitosis* as a type of cell reproduction that maintains the parental number of chromosomes in each daughter nucleus, and she presents on the screen in full view of each student a short video sequence of the process of mitosis. The sequence replays in slow motion as Professor Ross points out that the number of chromosomes is being maintained.

Professor Ross goes on to explain key components of the mitosis process, including chromosomal structures and microtubular structures. She defines each concept and then presents two to three images representing this concept on the front screen, pointing out key features. Following a question from a student, she returns quickly to a previously presented image and compares it to a more recent image.

In explaining the stages of mitosis, Professor Ross again uses the short video sequence that she had displayed previously, but now breaks up the sequence into its proper stages. She defines the first stage, called *prophase*, explains the emergence of the chromosomes as threadlike structures, and shows the section of the video sequence associated with this phase. Professor Ross continues her presentation with the metaphase, anaphase, and telophase stages of mitosis, each time defining the nature of the phase, using a video sequence to demonstrate the entire phase, and stopping the action in the sequence to demonstrate key points. To contrast between different phases she can quickly return to a previous stage and forward to a later stage.

This teaching method is made possible by using readily available and moderately priced equipment. The video images come from the BioSci II videodisc, which includes over 6,000 still images, 100 video sequences that can be used with or without narrative, and 500 computer graphic diagrams. A Pioneer 2200 player sends selected video images to the Eiko large screen projector, which was already in the auditorium. Professor Ross uses her own Macintosh Classic computer to create laser bar codes for the portion of the videodisc she wanted to use, and during the presentation she used a hand-held, bar-code reader to select portions of the videodisc. The BioSci II videodisc and the videodisc player are the only two system elements purchased specifically for the multimedia presentation. These two items cost $1400, and they can be used by many other instructors in numerous settings.

Scenario Number Two

Jim and Sue, both seniors majoring in teacher education, are serving as peer facilitators for small groups in their elementary education course. Both are using a computer program and videodisc application, *Understanding Groups*, to teach about group dynamics. The videodisc contains longer segments of behavior from six different groups and covers topics such as shared leadership, group goals, communication, and conflict resolution. Jim created an instructional design in which a definition is followed by an example, a so-called *deductive* design. Sue selected a variety of examples of group interaction from the many on the disc—such as in an elementary classroom, a college class, a senior citizens' advisory group, a drug treatment group, and a parent education group. She organized examples of similar group behaviors from which learners could develop their own labels and explanations—an *inductive* approach.

Jim starts his group by reviewing the material to be studied. He uses some initial computer screens that are projected with an LCD panel onto a large screen in the front of the classroom. He introduces a concept, such as managing a group, with a text definition on the computer screen and an audio definition from the videodisc, and then shares a video example of the concept on a television monitor alongside him. He repeats this instructional method for several other concepts, repeating the definition or showing another video example as students request. After showing the instructional part of the program, he shares video examples of interaction in another group and discusses the nature of the interaction before entering a group response on the computer. Jim ends the period by showing his classmates how to employ HyperCard so that they can create programs for other videodisc materials in their own classrooms.

Sue begins her session by showing the several segments of group interaction that she had selected. She leads a discussion about the common elements the group members saw in the segments and how they might be appropriately labeled. After students develop their own label, they view (via the video monitor) what an expert in group theory has to say about the interaction. Sue's classmates seem to be involved and to enjoy looking at the variety of group interaction segments from various groups. Like Jim, Sue also shows some aspects of programming and demonstrates how the computer can be used in an elementary classroom.

In debriefing with the instructor at the conclusion of the experience, Sue and Jim express their enthusiasm for the new technologies. To be able to bring such a variety of examples to learners, to have a common referent for discussion, to design different ways of approaching learning—all that seems positive from their perspectives. The learners in the small groups also indicate a positive response. They liked having a peer facilitator. The fact that a peer had completed the program and led the discussion made the new technologies less intimidating. All felt that they would use new interactive multimedia in their own teaching.

The videodisc application Jim and Sue used had been developed by a faculty research team on their own campus. Although they had no previous experience with programming, after an initial training period Jim and Sue had little difficulty using HyperCard to program the videodisc. HyperCard allowed them to use buttons and to create branching, to create text, and to connect the computer program with the videodisc player. In fact, the students often commented that they enjoyed seeing behind the scenes of the new technologies.

To prepare the hardware, Sue and Jim had to obtain the video monitor, a Macintosh Classic computer, a Pioneer 4400 videodisc player, and an overhead computer screen projector from the university's media resources center. It was a little complicated connecting all the cables, but they managed the job with a little help from a faculty member. They practiced their presentations beforehand and, despite some initial butterflies, completed them smoothly.

Scenario Number Three

Maria, a freshman student at a community college in rural California, uses a computer with a mouse to explore numerous aspects of a single work of literature—*Black Elk Speaks*, by John G. Niehardt. As she reads the book on the computer screen, Maria illuminates the text in a number of ways. When she encounters a term she does not understand, she highlights that word and clicks the mouse on a "hot button" to get its definition. Another option calls up video clips and graphics to provide both historical and cultural contexts for a particular passage. By clicking the mouse, she solicits multiple critical interpretations of sections or analyses of literary devices and patterns. Universal themes and patterns in the book are linked to other works when she selects that option. More than 180 hours of interactive explorations are available, but Maria uses only a small portion of this material, having to select thoughtfully those portions that enable her to complete her assignment.

Maria's exploration of *Black Elk Speaks* is made possible through the efforts of her instructor, John Washington, who teaches an introductory course on multicultural literature. Dr. Washington recognized that many of his students lacked some of the contextual background and literary analysis skills to understand some of the works that he assigned, so he explored new options for providing his students with the needed background and skills. He discovered that the Illuminated Books and Manuscripts multimedia application, developed by IBM and a business partner, provided learners self-selected opportunities to obtain necessary background information and the analytical skills to achieve the goals he had for his students.

After some initial exploration, Dr. Washington discovered that the Illuminated Books and Manuscripts application, and the IBM Ultimedia platform required to run this application, were quite expensive. The application itself cost about $2,000, and the IBM PS/2 computer with a CD-ROM drive, 160-MB hard drive, and other components, coupled with a XGA monitor and Pioneer LD-V8000 LaserDisc Player, cost about $9,000. Dr. Washington's request for funds from his department and college yielded only $2,000, but he applied for and obtained a grant that covered the needed funds from a regional foundation that was sympathetic to the philosophy of cultural diversity as a priority. After a successful pilot year, he obtained two additional Ultimedia platforms. Through careful scheduling in the multimedia service center at his college, he can now accommodate all of his students .

Comments on Scenarios

These scenarios center around the use of a new tool for education—interactive multimedia. The examples incorporate multimedia in the sense that they use a variety of media forms, including full-motion video, stills, graphics, text, and animation; and they represent the interactivity that is possible with multimedia. The interactivity takes the form of a teacher selecting and reselecting visual material in response to student questions, peer instructors providing instruction to accommodate different learning styles, and a student using only that portion of the instruction that she finds relevant.

The three scenarios also differ in significant ways. In the first scenario, Professor Ross uses an existing videodisc that was developed elsewhere as a teaching tool to enhance a classroom presentation after developing her own laser bar codes to facilitate quick random access to desired stills and video segments. In the second scenario, Jim and Sue use a videodisc developed by faculty on their own campus to teach their peers about group dynamics and to learn about a new learning technology in the process. The third scenario demonstrates how an individual student can use a multimedia application combining videodiscs, CD-ROM, digital video, computer graphics, and text that was developed by a vendor and made available to students through the efforts of a faculty member.

Making Scenarios a Reality

The need for new solutions for problems in higher education certainly exists. The hardware and the multimedia applications are available. The students are ready to learn in ways consistent with their preferred learning styles. The missing ingredient is knowledge about and interest in multimedia on the part of faculty members, many of whom seem reluctant to take advantage of these new interactive learning tools. Each of the three scenarios described above could be happening in a higher education classroom or learning center today.

Of equal importance, the research and evaluation conducted on the use of multimedia indicate its effectiveness in facilitating learning on a number of dimensions. DeBloois (1987) and Carlson and Falk (1991) summarize a variety of literature indicating the benefits of instruction centered around interactive video for education and training. Other researchers have concluded that multimedia is effective in enhancing content acquisition in chemistry (Smith & Jones, 1988), art (Phillips et al., 1988), pre-calculus (Henderson & Landesman, 1988), and teacher education (Carlson & Falk, 1991). Use of multimedia applications have also led to greater learner satisfaction (ibid.) and have the advantage of being able to match the student's learning style (Carlson, 1991).

Faculty members, administrators, and others involved in higher education must come to understand multimedia as the integration of computers, interactive video, CD-ROM, and/or other computer peripherals to facilitate interactive teaching and learning. Instructors must discover that in using multimedia as a teaching tool, they can integrate its various elements to develop interactive classroom presentations that are stimulating, informative, and flexible. They must understand as well that multimedia applications are viable as learning tools to provide tailored, self-paced, open-ended, interactive instruction for individual students or small groups of students outside of the classroom.

But more than knowing the capabilities of this new technology in solving educational problems, those involved in higher education must recognize multimedia as a process that they can begin to use in their own setting. This book is organized around using a problem solving orientation to (1) define current problems in higher education and in one's specific discipline, (2) examine multimedia as a significant set of solutions that can make opportunities out of current problems, (3) identify the potential niche of multimedia in higher education, (4) provide guidelines for the use of multimedia as a teaching and learning tool, and (5) propose how multimedia solutions can be evaluated to determine how effectively they have solved educational problems.

Overview

The following chapters are organized to provide practical information that will enable those interested in using multimedia in higher education to tap the potential of these new tools for interactive teaching and learning. Chapter 2 presents an instructional design process that uses a generic problem solving process as its foundation, and Chapter 3 defines more specifically the problems and opportunities surrounding the use of interactive multimedia in higher education.

Part II (Chapters 4 through 8) describes ways of generating new solutions to educational problems using multimedia. Chapter 4 introduces the hardware that enables new opportunities for teaching and learning. The manner in which hardware and applications can be integrated is described in Chapter 5, which focuses on new models and methods for using multimedia in higher education. Chapters 6, 7, and 8 describe three distinct ways of generating multimedia applications— buying existing applications, developing one's own applications from scratch, and repurposing existing materials.

In Part III, Chapter 9 provides information on deciding on how to use multimedia most effectively, exploring the niche that multimedia can fill as one significant teaching and learning tool among many that exist for higher education. Chapter 10 offers guidelines for using multimedia in classrooms and learning centers, and Chapter 11 describes how this use can be evaluated.

Part IV concludes the book. It looks at the future of multimedia in Chapter 12, and provides a summary and conclusion in Chapter 13.

Each chapter begins with a description of its goals and a rationale for why these goals must be achieved to develop or use multimedia in higher education. General information related to these goals is provided, based on the literature available on the topic and on the authors' experiences. The specific questions that each instructor must ask of oneself are then introduced. A case study describing how these questions have been answered previously is provided, and some general guidelines are proposed related to the topic. Finally, the reader is directed to additional resources, many of which are described in the appendix, and a conclusion of material in the chapter is presented.

Conclusion

Multimedia has the potential not only to improve current educational practices but to revolutionize the way that higher education is provided. Multimedia can make lectures more interesting and effective and, more so than books, can provide more varied information to students outside of class. Moreover, having the skills to use multimedia can empower students to learn in new ways and to develop higher-order cognitive skills.

It is particularly important that people in higher education seek ways to improve their productivity. Over the past two decades the cost of higher education has increased rapidly, but no evidence suggests that the outcomes for students have improved. In short, while other sectors of society have improved their productivity by the appropriate application of new technologies, productivity in higher education has suffered.

Multimedia represents a potentially powerful technology for higher education that could, with proper use, increase productivity immensely. The material in this book provides a solid foundation for instructors to incorporate multimedia appropriately as a new tool for teaching and learning in higher education—and thereby enhance productivity accordingly.

CHAPTER 2

PROBLEM SOLVING AS A GENERIC INSTRUCTIONAL DESIGN PROCESS

Goals

In order to integrate multimedia into instructional activities in higher education, one must undertake a systematic development process. Important steps in this process consist of: (1) define the educational needs that must be met; (2) examine possible ways that multimedia could be used to address these needs; (3) decide how to actually use the multimedia applications; (4) use the application; and (5) evaluate the extent to which the multimedia solution meets the educational need. This type of educational problem solving undertaken systematically, is usually termed *instructional design* or *instructional systems design*.

This chapter provides an overview of instructional systems design activities as a problem solving process that can be used to address educational needs using multimedia as at least part of the solution. Subsequent chapters elaborate on the activities and concepts introduced in the current chapter.

General Information

The Need for Instructional Design

Instruction at the university and other institutions of higher education in the Western tradition began about 1,000 years ago in cities such as Bologna and Paris. The methodology took the form of the instructor, or professor, lecturing to the students, with the students taking notes and the instructor testing the students to determine how well they had learned the material presented. About 500 years ago, books became available and gradually became the dominant tool used for instruction.

Thus, the traditional instructional process in higher education involved instructors, learners, and textbooks. The knowledge resided in the textbook, and the instructor was responsible for "teaching" that content to the students. The instructor's role was to select an appropriate text and then to get the content into students' brains in a way that the students could retrieve the information for a test. In this model, instruction improved if the teacher selected better

11

texts, expanded his or her knowledge of the content, and lectured better (Dick & Carey, 1985).

In more recent times, significant new tools became available to facilitate university instruction. Blackboards, overhead and slide projectors, and audiotapes and videotapes are some of the physical tools that have come into use. Additionally, small group discussions, case studies, simulations, and individualized curricula have been added as instructional strategies that can be used as tools to enhance teaching and learning. Significantly, multimedia not only combines the capabilities of all of these physical tools mentioned, but can facilitate the effective incorporation of each of the instructional strategies noted.

These new tools, together with the broadened goals of higher education, have greatly expanded the role of the instructor. Instructors must systematically select, develop, implement, and evaluate a variety of hardware tools and instructional strategies to enhance teaching and learning. Unfortunately, as Foa (1989) suggests, teachers in higher education are among the few professionals who rarely receive direct training or supervised experience in the practice of their profession (teaching). Imagine a surgeon having a thorough knowledge of anatomy but no training or experience in actually performing an operation!

Fortunately, instructional systems design provides a set of activities to guide instructors in developing appropriate teaching methods. This set of activities consists of: (1) identifying the instructional goal, (2) examining the educational setting, (3) identifying learner characteristics and entry behaviors, (4) specifying objectives for the learner, (5) anticipating a method to assess achievement of objectives, (6) developing an instructional strategy, (7) developing and selecting instructional materials, and (8) designing and conducting evaluations of the instruction (Dick & Carey, 1985; Seels & Glasgow, 1990).

Instructional systems design, however, can be more time consuming, rigorous, and tedious activity than most college instructors find practical. Consequently, this book adopts a more familiar conceptual framework for systematically developing instruction; namely, a problem solving process applied to education.

Instructional Systems Design as Problem Solving

Problem solving is a process involving the following steps: (1) defining the problem, (2) generating alternative solutions, (3) examining alternative solutions and selecting a solution, (4) implementing the solution selected, and (5) evaluating whether the solution solved the problem. Instructional systems design provides guidance for the type of activities that occur during each step. Figure 2.1 provides a graphic representation of the relationship of problem solving and instructional design.

Defining the Problem

Instructional design emphasizes systematically defining the educational problem to be solved prior to seeking solutions to that problem. Aspects of the prob-

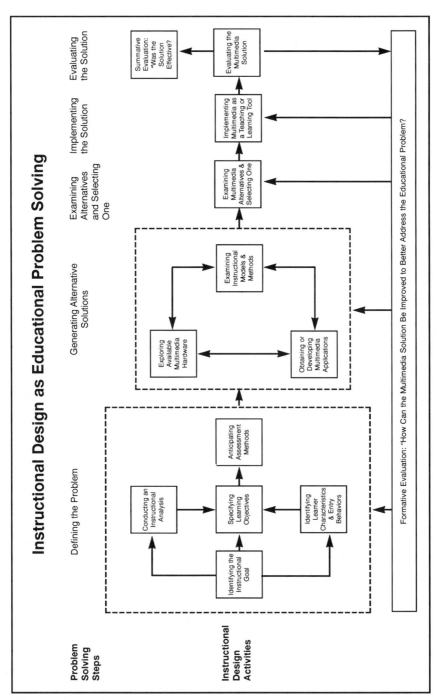

Figure 2.1

lem receiving particular attention consist of the following: (1) identifying the instructional goal, (2) examining the educational setting, (3) identifying learner characteristics and entry behaviors, (4) specifying learning objectives, and (5) anticipating a method of assessing whether objectives have been achieved (Dick & Carey, 1985; Seels & Glasgow, 1990).

Identifying the instructional goal. The first step in defining the problem is to determine what, in general, the instruction intends to achieve. The instructional goal may be derived from a needs assessment, standards that must be met for accreditation, the broad goals for higher education, or practical experience of what students will need to know in order to perform effectively in a particular job.

Analyzing the educational setting. After identifying the general goal for the instruction, it is important that one steps back and examines the context within which the instruction will occur. Factors to consider include the nature of the educational system in which the instruction will be provided, the general educational needs in that system, and the forces acting on the system.

Identifying learner characteristics and entry behaviors. You must identify any specific learners' characteristics that may be important in designing the instruction. And you must define the prerequisite knowledge and skills required to undertake the instruction, and assess the degree to which learners possess these skills.

Specifying learner objectives. Based on the previous two steps, you write out more specific statements on what the learner will be able to do following the instruction. These statements identify the knowledge and skills to be learned and the criteria for successful performance.

Anticipating a method of assessment. Prior to considering the type of instruction to be undertaken, you should consider how to assess whether the instruction to be developed achieved the objectives that were specified. Many instructional designers advocate development of criterion-referenced tests, but portfolio assessments, in which students put together a set of materials demonstrating that they have achieved certain objectives, or other less formal means of assessment, may be appropriate.

Generating Alternative Solutions

This step involves identifying and developing a variety of ways in which instruction could be provided to solve the educational problem identified above. Each instructor may have favorite solutions that they typically use. Some instructors may stick to traditional methods of asking students to read books and take tests while they provide lectures to expand upon and clarify the content from the book. Some instructors may emphasize the use of case studies that students read outside class and then discuss in class; others may make extensive use of cooperative activities in small groups. In reality, each instructor may use a variety of teaching tools and strategies to solve an identified educational problem.

This book emphasizes multimedia as an alternative set of solutions to a variety of educational problems. In order to generate alternative solutions involving multimedia, the instructor must know appropriate multimedia hardware options, understand how multimedia applications can be obtained or developed, and be aware of instructional models and methods for using multimedia applications.

Multimedia hardware. A variety of multimedia hardware is currently available, with new equipment and capabilities being introduced regularly. To address the educational problem that is identified, instructors need to understand the appropriate combinations of computers, videodisc players, CD-ROM drives, computer peripherals, and input and output devices.

Instructional design options. The overall instructional design includes describing the methods and models for using multimedia hardware and applications for instruction. In the broadest sense, two methods of instruction are possible—using multimedia as a *teaching tool*, where the instructor selectively uses specific aspects of an application to enhance her or his presentation or coverage of a particular topic in the context of a class; or as a *learning tool*, which involves a learner using a multimedia system and interacting with the instructional program in a self-directed manner. The models for instruction, all of which are defined in Chapter 5, include video-enhanced didactic presentations, exploration, structured observation, simulated personal interaction, and assessment and focused instruction.

Multimedia applications. Applications are the core of instruction that incorporates multimedia. These applications can be generated in three basic ways: (1) purchased off the shelf from another developer; (2) a portion (usually a videodisc or CD-ROM) purchased and then modified or repurposed to achieve desired goals and objectives; or (3) developed "from scratch." Each of these options are described below.

The authors believe that because college instructors typically know quite well the content of a course but receive no direct training, most teach pretty much as they were taught in college. Therefore, most instructors seldom consider multimedia as an alternative tool for solving educational problems. To provide instructors with the necessary background to consider multimedia, Chapters 4 through 8 focus on (1) the expanded teaching capabilities afforded by multimedia hardware, (2) the kinds of instruction possible with multimedia, and (3) the types of software applications that now can be obtained or developed.

Examining Alternative Solutions and Selecting One

After examining various potential solutions to an educational problem, the instructor must decide which solution will most effectively and efficiently solve the identified problem. With regards to multimedia, the instructor must first determine whether the solution(s) that incorporates multimedia offers advantages over other types of instruction and, therefore, should be selected for use. If multimedia solutions are selected, the instructor must determine the most effective method and model. Chapter 9 provides criteria, questions, and guidelines for examining advantages and disadvantages of multimedia and for deciding about whether and how to use multimedia for instruction.

Implementing the Solution Selected

Once the instructor has selected a particular solution, he or she must effectively implement that choice. Whatever the solution selected (lecturing, case study, small group discussion, etc.), the instructor must prepare to provide that instruction. Instruction involving multimedia involves special kinds of preparation and skills that are unfamiliar to most instructors, including emphasizing the interactivity inherent in quality multimedia applications. Chapter 10 includes information on how to prepare for and provide instruction using multimedia as both a teaching and learning tool.

Evaluating Whether the Solution Solved the Problem

Evaluation of multimedia, and all other forms of instruction for that matter, can take two primary forms—formative and summative. Formative evaluation actually occurs throughout the process of generating, selecting, and implementing solutions. It seeks to answer the question: How can this instruction be improved? Summative evaluation usually occurs after the instruction was implemented and seeks to answer the question: Did the instruction effectively achieve the goals for which it was intended?

Multimedia instruction requires special types of evaluation because of the uniqueness of the type of instruction that can be delivered and because this instructional tool is so new and has had limited foundation research. Chapter 11 includes questions and guidelines relevant to evaluating multimedia as an instructional tool and summarizes some of the previous evaluative research.

A Comparison Between Instructional Design and Traditional Instruction

Instructional systems design differs from the traditional approach along a number of dimensions. Systematic instruction emphasizes a more thorough definition of an educational problem before considering the instruction to be developed and offered. Specific goals and objectives are developed (often by both the instructor and students) and are known to both the instructor and students. These goals and objectives provide a base for developing an instructional strategy and for evaluating the degree to which the students and the instruction have succeeded in solving the problem. Learner characteristics and a careful analysis of the instruction are characteristic of instructional system design.

Instructional design also emphasizes the numerous alternatives available to teachers, with multimedia becoming an increasingly important and available option. In the United States traditional instruction at universities has been dominated by the lecture format, while in some other countries a tutorial format dominates. Evaluation of instruction of both a formative and summative nature is central in instructional systems design.

Questions

To apply the instructional design process described above to a particular setting, the following questions can be asked:

1. What is the nature of the educational problem we are trying to address?
   What is the general goal of the instruction?
   What is the nature of the setting for the instruction?
   What is the nature of the instructional task?
   What are the characteristics and entry behaviors of the learners?
   What specifically should the learners be able to do after the instruction?
   How might we assess whether the instructional strategy developed
   achieved the identified goals and objectives?

2. What types of solutions to these problems can be generated using multimedia?
   What can the hardware do?
   What software applications can be obtained or developed?
   What instructional models and methods can be used with multimedia?

3. What are the advantages and disadvantages of different forms of multimedia as solutions to educational problems?

4. What are key criteria to use in deciding whether to use multimedia as a teaching and learning tool?

5. How can multimedia solutions be implemented most effectively?
   —When used as a teaching tool?
   —When used as a learning tool?

6. How can multimedia be effectively evaluated as an educational tool?
   How can multimedia instruction be improved?
   Is multimedia instruction effective in achieving identified goals?

Example

The problem solving orientation of instructional systems design is exemplified by the development of a videodisc application on *Understanding Groups* undertaken by the Videodisc Research Group (VRG) at the University of Minnesota, Duluth, beginning in 1985. Each of the steps of problem solving, and the instructional design activities associated with it, are described below.

Defining the Problem

The initial step was to define the problem. The instructional design activities associated with this step were as follows:

Identifying the instructional goal. The instructional goal involved students in the College of Education and Human Service Professions (CEHSP). The intent was for those students to understand group dynamics and to apply this knowledge so that they could interact more effectively in groups. This goal was identified in talking to subject matter experts and through communications with individuals who employ CEHSP graduates.

To achieve the goal, the learners would need to be able to (1) understand numerous concepts related to group dynamics; (2) identify behaviors representing these concepts; and (3) choose appropriate behaviors in response to specific group situations. Other content areas related to shared leadership, group communication, group goals, and conflict resolution were identified as central to the instructional group; and leadership styles, group decision making, and power in groups were likewise targeted.

Analyzing the educational setting. The educational setting was a CEHSP at a medium-sized comprehensive university. Forces acting on the setting at the time included an increased pressure for efficiency in teaching and documenting effective outcomes for students. As a professional program, a need existed for development of specific skills important to the teaching role.

Identifying learner characteristics and entry behaviors. Learner characteristics and entry behaviors were identified by surveying potential learners. Among the distinctive characteristics identified was that some learners preferred to learn new material by a straightforward presentation leading directly toward what they needed to know; other learners preferred instruction enabling them to develop their own ideas about the nature of the information presented. While the target audience included both graduate and undergraduate students, a test on basic concepts of group dynamics indicated a relatively low level of comprehension of those concepts among both graduate and undergraduate students.

Specifying learner objectives. Based on the previous steps, objectives for the instruction were written. One performance objective emphasized understanding, and stated: "The learner will be able to identify the definition and video examples of the following shared leadership concepts: task behaviors, information seeking, managing." A second objective emphasized applying knowledge to choose appropriate group behavior, and stated: "After viewing a segment of group behavior, the learner will be able to identify missing shared leadership behaviors and select an appropriate behavior to improve the group's functioning."

Anticipating a method of assessment. Two methods of assessment were anticipated: a multiple choice test to determine whether students could identify definitions of key terms introduced in the instruction, and presenting video examples of specific concepts and asking students to identify the concepts. Both methods were subsequently used.

Generating Alternative Solutions

There are a number of alternative solutions to the educational problem of teaching students about group dynamics. This broad goal had previously been pursued through readings, lectures/discussions of key concepts in class, and role playing and observing group behaviors in class. Because the VRG wanted to pursue multimedia as a solution to this particular educational problem, three aspects of generating a solution, related to hardware, applications, and specifying the instructional design, were undertaken.

Multimedia hardware. In 1985 relatively few multimedia platforms existed. Our campus had just received fifteen state-of-the-art IVIS (interactive video information systems) units from Digital Equipment Company, and this equipment was selected as the hardware on which multimedia instruction could be delivered. Each unit comprises a DEC Pro 350 computer with a 10-MB hard disk, a Sony 1000a videodisc player, and a single monitor that displayed both the video from the videodisc and the text and graphics (including overlay) from the computer on a single screen. Other multimedia hardware could have been examined, but the IVIS equipment was a realistic choice because it was the only one available and there was little possibility of obtaining other hardware.

Instructional design options. A number of possible instructional designs were developed. One possibility included using a single case study to demonstrate and later apply group dynamics concepts. A second alternative included using computer text and audio to introduce and define key concepts and then use video segments of group behavior as examples of the concepts. A third possibility was to present learners with examples of group behaviors and then ask the learners to develop their own theories about the nature of these behaviors. Because of the nature of the hardware available at that time, only instruction that involved individual or small groups of learners interacting with the instructional program at the IVIS system were considered.

Multimedia applications. A survey of existing videodiscs indicated that no multimedia applications were available related to group dynamics in 1985, therefore CEHSP could neither purchase nor repurpose an existing application. The VRG therefore developed an application to achieve the instructional goals and objectives identified. The development process is described more fully in Chapter 7.

Examining Alternative Solutions and Selecting One

The solution ultimately selected included using the videodisc application as a learning tool, which enabled learners to select among two instructional models and to practice and apply the concepts that they learned. For each of four major topics (shared leadership, group goals, communication, conflict resolution), learners first took a pre-test to determine their entry level of knowledge. Those learners with less prior knowledge pursued one of two instructional tracks. The deductive track presented a specific concept with computer text and audio, defined the concept using the same media, and presented one or two short video examples of the concept from a six-minute demonstration group interaction. The inductive track presented a number of short video examples from the demonstration group, asked each learner to develop a theory about the nature of the interaction, received an "expert's" comments on the interaction, and asked the learners to compare and contrast their observations to those of the expert.

Following the instruction, or after scoring very well on the pre-test, learners practiced identifying examples of specific group behaviors exhibited in video segments from one of four practice groups. Learners received feedback on how effectively they identified examples of various concepts. After completing the practice activities, learners engaged in simulated interaction with five other group members that allowed them to apply what they had learned about a particular topic. Learners observed an initial video portion of group interaction, were asked to select from among three possible behaviors that could occur next, and then saw a video playout of what would happen as a result. Learners saw a positive playout only when they identified and selected an appropriate behavior that was based on concepts previously presented.

Implementing the Solution Selected

The multimedia application *Understanding Groups* was used in several courses. Pre-service education students used the application either as individuals or in pairs to learn about group dynamics in a teaching methods course. Psychology students were exposed to basic concepts in a group dynamics course. Graduate social work students used the application to obtain knowledge of concepts that would enable them to facilitate groups more effectively.

Evaluating Whether the Solution Solved the Problem

A number of evaluation studies were conducted on the use of the *Understanding Groups* application. Formative evaluations were actually conducted throughout the development process, with subject matter experts examining the goals, objectives, and instructional models and offering suggestions for improvement; learners also went through a preliminary version of one module, and changes in the computer program were made based on observations and written feedback from students.

Several summative evaluations were also conducted. These studies involved randomly assigning learners to different types of multimedia instruction and to more traditional forms of instruction on groups, and then measuring the degree to which goals and performance objectives were met. Results generally indicated that multimedia applications were superior to traditional methods of instruction on criteria such as knowledge acquisition and observational skills, and that different methods of multimedia instruction (didactic presentation or inductive exploration) led to different outcomes for different types of learners (Carlson & Falk, 1989; Carlson, 1991).

The case study above provides an example of undertaking instructional systems design activities within a problem solving process. Not all of the activities were thoroughly completed, all options for instruction were not explored, and sometimes the sequence of activities differed from the ideal. But the general process was most useful in organizing activities that led to effective instruction with multimedia.

Guidelines

1. Carefully define the problem before examining possible solutions. Identify as many aspects of the problem as possible from the following: the broad instructional goals, learner characteristics, the nature of the instruction, the learning objectives, and possible means of assessment.
2. Examine a number of possible solutions, including those that incorporate multimedia and those that do not, before deciding which one to adopt. Know the options involving multimedia that are available, including the capabilities of the hardware, the types of applications that can be obtained or developed, and the instructional models and methods that are possible with multimedia.
3. Carefully examine the advantages and disadvantages of each alternative before adopting a specific solution, or combination of solutions. Select an appropriate mix of multimedia hardware, applications, and instructional models and methods when this combination offers advantages over other alternatives of addressing the defined educational problem.
4. Implement a solution incorporating multimedia as appropriate. Use multimedia's interactive capabilities as either a teaching tool or a learning tool.
5. Evaluate whether the chosen multimedia solution effectively and efficiently achieved the goals that were specified as part of the defined problem. Throughout the design and development process, examine how the instruction could be improved.

Resources

A number of excellent resources are available to facilitate effective instructional design and therefore facilitate educational problem solving using multimedia. Books on instructional design by Johnson and Foa (1989); Dick and Carey (1985); Reigeluth (1983); Seels and Glasgow (1990); Leshin, Pollock, and Reigeluth (1992); Schwier and Misanchuk (1993); and Kemp (1985) present relevant information on instructional design, which may be used as a basis for incorporating multimedia into instruction. Books by DeBloois (1985), Iuppa (1990), and Iuppa and Anderson (1988) more specifically address the instructional design principles involved in designing multimedia applications.

Several journals regularly address instructional design topics. *Educational Technology* has numerous recent articles on the relationship of instructional design to educational technology. *Educational Technology Research and Development* and *Multimedia Review* also include articles on instructional design as it relates to multimedia.

Numerous conferences include significant tracks on instructional design. SALT (The Society for Applied Learning Technologies) sponsors two conferences per year—Orlando, Florida, in late February and in Washington, D.C., in late August—that address both multimedia and instructional design. The AECT (Association for Educational Communications and Technology) holds its annual national convention in February, with a significant portion of the sessions focusing on current issues in instructional design.

Individuals and departments of instructional design are increasingly found on college and university campuses. A visit to any campus that has such resources may prove very fruitful. People knowledgeable about instructional design and multimedia are usually enthusiastic about their work and quite willing to share their knowledge and experiences with others.

Conclusion

Adopting a problem solving process and undertaking a number of instructional design activities can provide an excellent framework for developing and using multimedia as an effective teaching and learning tool. This same process and set of activities works for an instructional unit of almost any size—from a portion of a class session to an entire curriculum. Usually, the larger the scale of the unit of instruction, the more intensive the instructional design activities will be.

It is often impractical for university faculty to undertake a full-blown instructional systems design process to decide how to teach each course, let alone each class session or general topic. Following a more general problem solving process and incorporating a knowledge of multimedia and selected instructional design activities could allow instructors to incorporate multimedia as appropriate and to improve their instruction in general. The chapters that follow expand on each step of the problem solving process and on the instructional design activities presented in this chapter.

CHAPTER 3

DEFINING THE PROBLEM

Goals

A key element of instructional design and problem solving is the ability to define clearly and accurately the nature of an educational problem. This chapter provides educators with information on the dimensions to examine when trying to define educational problems and to provide general data on these dimensions as it now relates to higher education.

General Information

Higher education is undergoing rapid change and faces a variety of challenges. The information provided below should help in understanding the context within which problems related to teaching and learning can be defined; it also provides a framework for analyzing how multimedia can help improve teaching and learning.

The three key steps in defining the educational problem identified in the previous chapter are as follows: (1) describing the context of the higher education setting, (2) identifying learner characteristics and entry behaviors, and (3) identifying general goals and objectives for the instruction. Each of these components is explained more thoroughly below, together with information relevant to undertaking these activities in higher education. Before moving into the steps, we will examine some aspects of today's higher education setting.

The Setting in Higher Education

General education has taken on an expanded meaning. It now defines a process that is lifelong, consisting of not only preschool, regular school, and higher education, but the less formal educational opportunities that are proliferating both in and out of the workplace.

The International Standard Classification of Education was originally developed in the early 1970s to help clarify the various aspects of education. This definition, at the broadest level, encompasses experiential learning such as by doing and by self-direction. It includes informal education that happens through family living in a particular society, and which is heavily influenced by the popular media. Nonformal education includes out-of-school and continuing education

23

through on-the-job training. Formal education includes regular school (first and second levels comparable to elementary and secondary education in the United States) and higher or third-level education. Formal training in the acquisition of skills for employment in a specific occupation is called vocational education (UNESCO, 1991).

This book focuses on only one aspect of this broad educational scene—formal education at the university, or third, level. Usually this type of education takes place on a specific campus but is sometimes provided through various distance education programs.

Analyzing the Context of Higher Education

Need for productive work force. Current population trends in the industrialized countries include a rise in the total dependent populations (both younger children and older adults) relative to the working population. This situation demands increased productivity among working populations and requires continuous improvement of broad competencies, abilities, and understandings. More older adults, for example, are now enrolled in university education than ever before (ibid.).

Need for full employment. In times past, the transition from formal education to the world of work was often smooth. Not today. High levels of unemployment are endemic in both the developing and industrialized countries. For example, the number of unemployed in Western Europe soared from 2.5 million in 1970 to over 16 million in 1987, with unemployed youths accounting for 40 percent of the total. Increasing proportions of people in both Eastern and Western Europe enter jobs in which their education is not fully utilized. Third-level university graduates often displace second level graduates and bump them into lower level jobs. Because of the uncertain relationship between education and the world of work, universities are forging links with business and industry in various ways. These links often affect the nature of the curriculum (ibid.).

Need for adequate finances. The majority of countries in sub-Sahara Africa and in Latin American and the Caribbean area are enduring declines in the real growth of GNP, and many of those countries have cut back on public expenditures for education. The lessening of support has been greatest at the third level. Problems in public expenditure for education are unlikely to be solved until regional economies recover from the widespread collapses of the late 1980s. Likewise, in Europe, North America, and the former Soviet Union, the funding for higher education has decreased.

At the same time, in the United States, tuition in public institutions increased from $599 in 1975 to $2,006 in 1990; in private institutions the respective figures are $2,614 to $10,400. Student financial assistance through the Department of Education increased during the 1980s, but it fell by almost $65 million from 1989 to 1990 (Bureau of the Census, 1991). During an economic recession in which less funds are available for higher education despite increased tuition, it is anticipated that students will find it increasingly difficult to pay for their post-secondary education.

Need for various delivery models. Most countries have moved to a common general education at the second level while postponing specialization to the post-secondary levels. The mode of access to the universities has been different. In North America and Asia access, in principle at least, has been available to all graduates of second-level schools. In Europe, entry has been open only to graduates from a specific class of schools, and often even then, through competitive examination.

These traditional patterns are changing. There are now nontraditional open universities, community colleges, and distance learning. These systems have added flexibility to the university. For example, aborigines in remote areas of Australia who may not have had second-level education, now access higher education through multimedia distance learning courses with help from local tutors (Brady and Santo, 1992). Again, the impact on curriculum format has been extensive.

Need for broad understanding and humanistic learning. The changing definitions of literacy reflect the increasing complexity of the world and conceptions of learning. The original literacy definition—being able to read and write a short simple statement about one's everyday life—has been expanded. Three distinct types have been identified by Barton & Kirsch (1990): (1) prose literacy—the ability to read and interpret prose at advanced levels; (2) document literacy—the ability to identify and use information in such forms as tables, charts, and indices; and (3) quantitative literacy—the ability to understand and use numbers in all aspects of life.

Closely tied to this third type of literacy is a fourth area—technological and problem solving literacy. The need exists for learning to meet the needs of a swiftly changing society and rapidly developing technological environments. For example, even in the remote areas of China in which industrial enterprises run higher education vocational schools, it was found necessary to move beyond narrow skills training to broader education (Meng, 1989).

Even though higher education has become a critical factor in economic competition, there is also concern for a humanistic vision. Scholars have lamented the "closing of the American mind" through educational practices deemed too narrow to develop students capable of understanding the world about them (Bloom, 1987; Moore, 1990).

Need for accountability and assessment of learning outcomes. The assessment of learning achievement of students at the university is the subject of much debate. Where resource constraints limit the number of individuals selected for a course of study or for a work position, norm-referenced testing is used. Professors who simply need to know whether students have acquired the necessary prerequisite knowledge and skills use criterion-referenced, curriculum-based assessment methods. Assessment strategies for complex behaviors include portfolio creation and evaluation (Wolf et. al., 1991). Already, computer programs are used to document components of the portfolio and include the scanning of student work into that folio. The type of exit testing and assessment used can greatly influence the nature of the curriculum. This is no less true in higher education than at primary and secondary levels. Within this context, we address the process of instructional design for multimedia.

Summary of context. In summary, this book focuses on formal education at the third, or university, level. Key current needs include increased productivity for the work force and in the educational setting. Higher education must provide new delivery models, broad understanding, and humanistic learning with accountability and assessment. Multimedia, if it is to be an effective instructional tool in higher education, must address these current needs.

Identifying Learner Characteristics

Numerous general characteristics provide information about students currently involved in higher education. The factors described below indicate important dimensions to consider in understanding characteristics of students in local campuses.

Growth of numbers. In virtually all regions of the world over the past two decades, enrollment in third-level or university education has grown faster than in second-level or high school education. University enrollments (although starting from a low initial base) have exploded in some areas—quadrupling in sub-Sahara Africa, Eastern Asia, and Oceania, and trebling in the Arab states and Latin America. In North America, Europe, and the former Soviet Union, growth rates were about 50 percent. Growth slowed somewhat during the 1980s, but was generally higher in developing than developed nations. In absolute numbers, as many students are now enrolled in university education in the developing countries of Eastern and Southern Asia as there are in Europe, the former Soviet Union, and North America (UNESCO, 1991). Current projections suggest only a slight increase in full-time students in the United States by the year 2000—from just over seven million in 1985 to 7.9 million in the year 2000 (Bureau of the Census, 1991).

The make-up of the student body also continues to change. For example, in the United States the composition of the student body in higher education is drastically different than it was twenty to thirty years ago. More people are completing a college education, and diversity in race, class, age, and gender among the college population is increasing.

Older students. While the numbers of male students aged 18 to 24 remained about the same from 1982 to 1989 (almost 6 million), the number of those aged 35 and over has greatly increased (365 thousand in 1972 to 716 thousand in 1989). The number of female students has increased in both categories—for 18- to 24-year-olds, from 2.7 million in 1972 to 4 million in 1989; for those aged over 35 years, from 418 thousand in 1972 to 1.4 million in 1989 (ibid.).

Students from culturally diverse backgrounds. A complex relationship exists between the educational setting and the cultural environment of the learner. As more and more people from diverse groups within a particular society enter higher education, there is increased concern for instruction in multiple languages and from multiple perspectives. In the United States in 1960, only 7.7 percent of all persons completed a four-year college degree; by 1989 this rate had increased to 21.1 percent. Among African-Americans, only 2.1 percent completed such a program in 1960; by 1989 this figure was 11.8 percent. In 1970 only 3.2 percent of Hispanic women completed college, but by 1989, this figure stood at 8.8 percent. Of American Indian students completing high school in 1972, 56.1 percent had a four year college degree by 1986. The numbers of students from foreign countries has also increased. For example, only 179,000 students from Africa were enrolled in 1976; in 1989 there were 366,000. Asian students have increased from 97,000 to 232,000 (ibid.).

Gender issues. In most regions of the world, females are under-represented at every level of education. The percentages of female students relative to male students, however, has improved in university-level education, especially in Latin America/Caribbean, North America, Europe and the former Soviet Union (UNESCO, 1991).

More specifically, in the United States the percentages of female graduates in various programs has changed. In 1972, only 41 percent of university graduates were female; by 1988 that figure was over 68 percent. In the physical sciences, female enrollment increased from 13.8 percent to 30.4 percent, and in business and management from 9.1 percent to 46.7 percent. However, in computer and information sciences the percentage of female doctorates has declined, from 21.2 percent in 1972 to 11.2 percent in 1988 (Bureau of the Census, 1991).

Students with special needs. Many countries are now tending to include students with special needs into the regular setting. In some countries, this trend has extended beyond the first and second levels of education to the third level. For example, Section 402 of Public Law in the United States mandates that services be provided to college students with documented learning, physical mobility, emotional, and speech and language disabilities. Universities across the country have developed support centers to comply with the law.

Students with differing developmental levels, learning styles, and beliefs. University students vary greatly in their developmental levels, learning styles, and beliefs. Ways to meet these individual differences is one of the challenges of teaching adults.

College students often are at different developmental levels. At first, students see various elements of the world as either right or wrong; these students seek to find the right answer and repeat it on a test. Next, they move into more relativistic thinking and may believe that "anything goes"—if no absolutes exist in the world then one position is as good as another. Later, students begin to appreciate that all evidence is not of equal value in supporting conclusions. Finally students move into commitment. Here, even though the world is relativistic, students make choices and move forward even in the midst of uncertainty (King et. al., 1983; Moore, 1983; Perry, 1970; Van Cleaf, 1988).

McCarthy (1990) has studied how people learn by observing how they perceive and process information. From this work, she has described four major learning styles: *imaginative learners* seek to make connections between the academic world and the real world; *analytic learners* enjoy combining details to create theories and seek intellectual competence; *common sense learners* like to work with real problems that are of immediate use; and *dynamic learners* learn through trial and error in real experiences. These styles parallel those developed by Kolb (1981), who has also documented four different adult learning styles: abstract conceptual, concrete experiential, reflective observational, and active experimental. Because students like to pursue learning in diverse ways, the academic setting, with its common abstract lecture format, can be frustrating.

Students also vary according to preferred learning mode. Some students learn best from auditory means—lectures and verbal discussions. Other students need visuals to enhance their learning. Visual experience from television and videos dominates life in the United States today—even young children average over twenty-seven hours of television per week (re:act, 1984). Today, many students in higher education expect the familiar, passive, fast-paced presentation of these visual media. Finally, some students learn best through kinesthetic experience, where they can handle the materials and learn through various sources.

The political orientation of entering freshmen has changed over time. For example, in the United States in 1970, 34 percent declared themselves to be liberal, compared with only 22 percent in 1989. Conservative and middle-of-the-road viewpoints increased during that time. There were also differences in beliefs about other societal issues. In 1970, 48 percent of entering freshmen agreed that the activities of married women were best confined to home and family. Only 26 percent agreed with that idea in 1989. In 1970, 56 percent of freshmen felt that capital punishment should be abolished; less than two decades later, only 21 percent agree (Bureau of the Census, 1991).

Summary of Learner Characteristics. Increasingly, students in higher education are more diverse—more older students, more cultural differences, more females, as well as more students with special needs. In addition, students exhibit different learning styles, modes of learning, and developmental levels. To be effective, multimedia must address the needs of the varieties of learners found in higher education.

Identifying General Goals and Objectives for Higher Education.

In general, the goals for higher education are varied and extensive. In order to provide a list of goals that have potential relevance for a particular local setting, information about both international and national goals are presented below.

International goals. At the international level, broad educational goals had been identified as early as 1974 (UNESCO, 1974). These guiding principles include (1) an international dimension and a global perspective in education at all levels and in all its forms; (2) an understanding and respect for all peoples including their cultures, civilizations, values (including domestic ethnic cultures and cultures of other nations); (3) an awareness of the increasing global interdependence between peoples and nations; (4) abilities to communicate with others; (5) an awareness not only of the rights but also of the duties for individuals, social groups, and nations towards each other; (6) an understanding of the necessity for international solidarity and cooperation; and (7) a readiness to participate in solving the problems of community, county, and the world at large, particularly in areas such as the environment.

National goals. Based on the context previously described above for the United States, the goals for higher education emerge into five clusters. They reflect the current conflict between forces that promote a single societal/world view and forces that view the world from a pluralistic perspective with varieties of beliefs. The five clusters consist of (1) citizenship and social commitment/action, (2) research as a force for both change and continuity, (3) economic preparation for a vocation, (4) curriculum as liberal education from either a multicultural or a western tradition perspective, and (5) literacy abilities. More than ever before these goals must be attained with a minimum of scarce financial resources.

Regarding citizenship, Swift (1990) discusses the role of higher education in helping students become better citizens through exploration and service in the economic, social, political, and financial aspects of a community. Waterous (1989) emphasizes the use of knowledge for individual and social betterment. Martel (1988) provides a discussion of higher education's role in moving from a nation at risk to a nation of progress through goals that stress community regeneration. Morse (1989) discusses civic education goals as they relate to such areas as community and public service, studies of leadership, and civic or public leadership education.

Rice (1991) suggests that research efforts in the university include the following goals: (1) focus on both analytical theory building and knowledge gained through experience; (2) reintegrate specialized knowledge through interdisciplinary approaches; (3) address the pragmatic needs of the larger world; and (4) emphasize a scholarship of teaching and teaching methods.

Improvement of economic conditions, another goal area, is one function of higher education, particularly in developing countries that do not have the luxury of a separate institution for intellectual contemplation like that found in Western models. There must be a mega-science in which government and industry work together to bring rationality in decision making to improve the human condition through vocational preparation (Altbach 1991).

Pertaining to employment, Hsu (1990) describes higher education as one of the primary means of access to economic well being and upward mobility. Moore (1990) ties economic well-being to the learning outcomes movement and accountability; learners must be able to do something with what they know. The goal of higher education is promotion of the formulation of a global, multidisciplinary interpretation of development, a complex curriculum that combines training and research, study and productivity, tradition and progress, attachment to personal identity, and responsiveness to the world.

The foci for curriculum forms another area for consideration. Adelman (1989) suggests that study for all college students (including those in technical fields such as engineering) include minority and women's studies, popular culture/media, non-Western culture and society as well as Western culture and society—all are necessary to prepare college graduates for participation in the diverse world culture and economy. These goals are echoed by Rendon (1989) in stating that minority cultures and perspectives must be included in the college class. In summarizing criticism of Bloom's *Closing of the American Mind,* Reitz (1988) suggests that curriculum goals include a multicultural and world/historical perspective on social reality through the comparative study of social, natural, intellectual, and art history. Husen (1991) describes curriculum goals from the National Advisory Board and Grants Committee of the University in the United Kingdom. Goals should include an emphasis on underlying intellectual, scientific, and technological principles rather than on the provision of narrowly conceived specializations. There is need for an ethos of inquiry and the pursuit of truth.

Regarding literacy, Williams and Colby (1991) cite the nation's goals for the year 2000, including literacy in every adult American. This goal greatly affects curricula in community colleges, which are assuming the role of literacy provision. Tohme (1990) discusses the goals that universities must embrace in the struggles against illiteracy—both of a social and of a functional nature.

In summary, tension results from the desire of scholars to have elbow room to pursue truth for its own sake or to engage in basic research without market considerations, and the need for the university to be tied with business and government to pursue economic revitalization. There is tension between the tremendous need for access to education for peoples across the world (either through inflated requirements for work or because of genuine need to understand so much more in today's technological world) against the need to maintain a high quality of instruction, which usually diminishes with increases in the number of students. Tensions also exist between the liberal arts curricula and the pragmatic goals of learning a marketable skill and getting a job; tensions between competence and equity, equality and quality; tensions between accountability with very specific outcomes and the broader preparation for living in the world with its problem solving, scientific approaches and holistic/intuitive approaches. Multimedia, with its diverse application possibilities, has the potential to address these issues.

Conclusion

After considering the world and national settings for higher education, the general nature of the learners, and the broad goals of higher education, one must analyze the specific setting in which to develop instruction. If the higher education is vocational in nature, the development of skill-related instruction for specific employment could be important. If, on the other hand, the setting emphasizes humanistic liberal education, the ability to incorporate examples representing cultural diversity could be significant. If the learners have special needs, numerous helpful technologies could be utilized.

Upon analysis of the setting, it is helpful to consider the nature of the learners and to develop overall goals for one's teaching. For example, overall goals might focus on helping students prepare for the practical world, to become critical thinkers with analytical abilities, or to develop broad theoretical underpinnings for action. These broad goals can serve as both a basis for developing specific objectives and as a "reality check" for the types of learning experiences one has prepared. These overall directions give a sense of coherence and purpose to teaching and learning in higher education.

Questions

1. What is the nature of the higher education setting in which you are involved?

   Do needs for employment and a productive work force dominate?

   How do the levels of finances impact your setting?

   Are new service delivery models emerging that might be used in your course?

   How dominant are the forces for humanistic and broad understanding at your campus?

   What kinds of accountability are emerging?

   What function does higher education serve in your region?

   How does higher education relate to the broader world setting?

2. What are the most important characteristics of the learners in your higher education setting?

   What are the ages, gender, race, and learning abilities of your students?

   What are their learning styles?

   How distinctive are they as a whole?

   Along what dimensions are they different from one another?

3. What are the goals of your instruction?

   How do they relate to overall national and international goals of education?

   How do the broad goals of international understanding, citizenship and social action, research and critical thinking, economic improvement, and curriculum for diversity influence goals in your instruction?

4. In general, what kind of instruction is required to achieve the goals identified above?

What instructional models and methods of delivery would be most effective?

What principles provide a general coherence for one's instruction?

How can these principles affect the development of multimedia instructional programs?

Example

The authors' experience at their own institution provides examples of relevant dimensions to consider in defining the educational problem that a reader may address. The following example describes the process of analyzing the context of the instructional setting and the characteristics of the learner, as well as the process for developing general goals and objectives.

Analyzing the Context of the Instructional Setting

A midwestern university campus has approximately 7,500 students in five colleges—fine arts, business, science and engineering, liberal arts, and education and human service professions. As is true for many institutions of higher education, the college that prepares students for various human service professions suffered critical financial problems. No longer was it possible to offer instruction in the time-honored seminars, where small numbers of students learned professional skills under the tutelage of a professor. Student populations in courses were rising to the point that the college found it increasingly difficult to provide the individualized instruction needed to prepare skilled and sensitive professionals.

To address this problem, the college administration decided to secure funding to try a new approach that, in the long run, would prove cost effective. Administrators and faculty explored a variety of possible new configurations to offer instruction; of those considered, the most promising appeared to be level III interactive videodisc technology. To create individualized approaches to gaining professional competence, application was made for a grant to gain support for using this emerging technology. The funding agencies contacted were intrigued by the multimedia approach suggested, and the grant proposal was approved.

Analyzing the Learner Characteristics

After reviewing national and international trends in student demographics and learning characteristics, the planners developed a needs assessment tool for use with students pursuing careers in education and human service professions. Results of the demographic survey indicated some areas of similarity with broader trends and some areas of difference. Twenty percent of the respondents were male and 80 percent female; this was largely due to the dominance of females in social work and teacher education programs within the college. Five percent of the students were American Indian; one percent African-American; and one percent Southeast Asian (Hmong). These percentages reflect the upper midwestern area that produces most of the students. Twenty percent of the students were considered "nontraditional" (older than twenty-two years). Two students had officially documented special needs.

Students were surveyed to determine their learning style. The survey used twenty-five statements with a Likert scale, and the questions were based on the work of learning style theorists. A factor analysis of the responses yielded two groups—those students who wished to have clear directions and processes (deductive learner style), and those students who wished to create their own concepts and generalizations from various data sources (inductive learner style). All students indicated their preference for concrete examples and small group discussion. Thirty percent of the students were "high" auditory learners, while 40 percent were high "visual" learners.

The survey results suggested that the significant diversity in both demographics and learning characteristics would need to be considered in developing the instructional program. The capability to bring in concrete examples from a multicultural perspective and in visual format would be appealing to this group of learners.

Developing General Goals and Objectives

The general goals for higher education at the international and national levels were reviewed. In addition, campus goals were considered. The following general goals are listed in the university's bulletin: (1) development of the art of critical thinking; (2) examination of basic values in light of the thought and experience of humankind; (3) preparation for leadership and social responsibility, including tolerance for the ideas of others; (4) encouragement of broad cultural and intellectual interests; (5) development of effective communication abilities; and 6) development of vocationally useful skills. Two goal areas selected for emphasis were the development of analytical, critical thinking abilities as applied in human service situations and the acquisition of the skills needed to work successfully in a human service setting.

In order to have the students gain both a strong theoretical background and practical, on-the-job skills, a group of subject matter experts were surveyed. The group consisted of professors and administrators, and practitioners in human service settings. The results of the survey were tabulated and discussed with an "advisory board" consisting of representatives from the various human service professions. From those results emerged the general goals of applying the problem solving process to a case study developed from the current needs in the field. Interwoven into the case study would be specific skills in consulting with appropriate community agencies, knowing current laws and legal issues, and developing client-centered "treatment" plans. At this point, the definition of the problem phase of the process merged with the next steps of generating alternatives, defining solutions, and evaluating the results (all of which are discussed in later chapters).

Further Development of Instructional Program

Decision points in the multimedia instructional program were developed that would allow the learner to assume the role of a human service worker. Individualized feedback in the program would allow tutoring based on the learner needs. Different styles would be accommodated through alternative ways of accessing information—from a directory of human service professionals to a "dial-an-information" feature. Information was available in both visual and auditory fashion. Inductive learners could build data and arrive at generalizations; deductive learners could consult a glossary of concepts and examples.

A general outline of a case involving a teenager who was both pregnant and abused was developed by the development team and the advisory board. The outcome of the case depended on the decisions made by the learner in the role of a human service worker. The details of developing the multimedia instructional program as well as well as implementation and evaluation followed the procedures described in Chapters 7, 9, and 10.

Guidelines

In defining the problem, the following steps need to be considered:

1. Reflect on the nature of the setting in which you are involved in higher education. Clarify the function that the institution serves and your role within that institution.
2. Reflect on the characteristics of learners currently enrolled in higher education institutions. Determine the make-up of the student body you serve—gender, age, ability, race, ethnicity—and what that means for your instruction. Determine the learning styles of students you serve and how these needs could be met with diverse instructional formats and sequences.
3. Reflect on the general goals for higher education from international, national and local perspectives. Determine the general goals for your instruction.
4. Develop some specific goals and objectives and a beginning plan for instruction.

Resources

Readers can obtain more information about the instructional problems they face. General information about the nature of higher education can be obtained from UNESCO publications such as the World Education Reports and current publications from the Bureau of the Census, United States Department of Commerce. *The Learner Style Inventory* by Kolb (1985) is available from the McBer Company, Boston, Massachusetts; while *The Hemispheric Mode Indicator* by McCarthy (1986) is available from the Excell Company, Barrington, Illinois. General goals for higher education are summarized in research articles and national, state, and campus bulletins and reports.

Increasingly, general goals and competencies for higher education are being articulated across institutions in a particular state. *The Minnesota Transfer Curriculum,* an example of such an articulation, is available from the Higher Education Coordinating Board of the State of Minnesota.

Conclusion

When defining an instructional problem, it is important to consider the context and setting in which the instruction will occur. The needs for vocational and broad liberal education as well as citizenship and literacy may influence the types of instruction desired. Determining the characteristics of learners also is beneficial in designing not only the general framework for instruction but the examples and methods that will be used. Reviewing international, national, and local goals ties together the various strands of instructions into a coherent whole. In the example, all three of these dimensions were important in the creation of appropriate multimedia materials. In addition, it is important to develop goals with the support of community and university subject matter experts. Carefully defining the educational problem provides solid bases for examining multimedia educational solutions, which we explore in the next part of this book.

PART 2

Generating Multimedia Solutions

Part 2 focuses on how multimedia can provide various solutions to the educational problems identified in Part 1. Computer technology's amazing capabilities have made multimedia instruction possible, and it is important to have at least a general understanding of the nature and capabilities of computer-based equipment. Certain kinds of instructional models and methods for use are particularly suited to multimedia hardware, so it is also important to understand those aspects of the technology.

Multimedia hardware can be combined with instructional models and uses in three distinct and powerful forms of applications in higher education. First, the acquisition of an existing multimedia application is the most cost-effective way to generate a multimedia solution to an educational problem. Second, you can generate a multimedia solution by developing your own application "from scratch," complete with video and audio production. Third, if elements of existing multimedia applications are present but they cannot be adopted in their existing form, you can repurpose those elements into an application that focuses on the relevant educational problem.

Chapter 4 provides an overview of multimedia hardware and its functions. Capabilities include full-motion video, almost limitless still images, high-quality audio, computer text and graphics, huge amounts of data, and animation—all randomly and almost instantly available. Multimedia formats include videodiscs, CD-ROM, digital video, and a variety of other digital devices. IBM and compatible and Apple Macintosh computers are described as the core of multimedia hardware, with videodisc players, CD-ROM drives, and peripheral devices for inputting and outputting information also examined.

Chapter 5 describes models of instruction and methods of use that are especially appropriate for multimedia teaching and learning. Instructional models include video-enhanced didactic presentations, exploration, structured observation, simulated personal interaction, assessment, and focussed instruction. Methods of using multimedia are categorized as follows: as a *teaching tool*, where video, still images, audio, computer text and graphics, and animation can be incorporated into classroom instruction; or as a *learning tool*, where these same capabilities are incorporated into instruction to individuals or small groups at computer learning stations outside of class.

Chapter 6 describes sources for existing multimedia applications and a process for reviewing these applications. Sources include vendors and distributors, publishers, and other universities. The process for reviewing existing applications includes reviewing the educational goal, obtaining and reviewing the application, and examining the applications' models of instruction and potential uses. Examples of applications in a variety of disciplines are provided.

Chapter 7 explains the process and roles involved in developing a new multimedia application in a higher education setting. The development process includes specifying an instructional design, producing and mastering the videodisc or other multimedia form, and completing a computer program to address the educational problem. The development roles include manager, instructional designer, production specialist, computer programmer, and evaluator.

Chapter 8 describes the process of developing a repurposed multimedia application. This process involves identifying overlap between a particular educational problem and the contents of multimedia elements, and then using a specialized instructional design and a computer program to integrate the multimedia elements into a coherent application that addresses the instructional goals and objectives identified.

Each of the chapters described above follows a similar format. Goals for the chapter and general background and information are provided. Questions to guide the reader are presented, and specific case examples clarify the general information presented earlier. Guidelines and resources to consider in pursuing the topic of each chapter are also included.

CHAPTER 4

GENERATING SOLUTIONS: MULTIMEDIA HARDWARE

Goals

To use multimedia as an effective educational tool, one must understand some of the capabilities that the new technologies offer. This chapter intends to provide its readers with background information on the nature of these new technologies and with the framework and resources to identify and develop multimedia resources on their campuses.

While all aspects of multimedia are changing rapidly, hardware is the most dynamic area. This chapter provides the most up-to-date information available in 1994; but readers should consult with some of the resources listed at the end of this chapter for updates to this information. Much of the information in this chapter is based on sources such as Helsel (1990), Galbreath (1992a), and the *Multimedia Source Guide: Special Supplement to T.H.E. Journal* (1994).

General Information

An amazing range of hardware is available to provide instruction with multimedia, and the technology continues to expand rapidly. Consequently, it is difficult to provide current comprehensive information about the choices available. The approach in this chapter provides an overview of the variety of multimedia platforms that are currently available, but then focuses on the most accepted and stable of these technologies. It emphasizes capabilities of the technologies, particularly as they relate to use in an educational setting, rather than attempting to explain how the technology works.

Overview of Multimedia Hardware Capabilities

This chapter is by far the most technical in the book. Because it may offer more technical information than some readers want, the section overview summarizes the most basic information so that the reader can skim through the rest of the chapter if desired.

Multimedia functionality provides remarkable capabilities for education. The equipment used can store and present still images, full-motion video, high-quality stereo audio, text, graphics, and animation. Complex, yet easy-to-use, instructional programs can integrate any combination of these elements into a cohesive program. Different elements can be randomly accessed almost instantaneously. In essence, multimedia hardware can provide a single educational tool that integrates the capabilities of (1) a random access VCR, (2) a random access slide projector with thousands of slides, (3) a random access audiotape or CD audio player, (4) an electronic blackboard, and (5) a computer. These capabilities are all available simultaneously.

The material below describes different types of multimedia platforms (configurations of equipment), recognizing that digital technologies that can store all types of information on a computer disc are becoming more popular. The components of multimedia systems, including computers, videodisc players, CD-ROM drives, and input and output (I/O) devices are also explained.

Overview of Multimedia Platforms

Multimedia platforms have many configurations and forms, but they serve two basic functions: for *developing a multimedia application* that can later be used in the teaching and learning process; and for *delivering the multimedia instruction* to the learners. Different types of platforms that can be used as development or delivery systems are described below and summarized in Table 4-1.

Interactive video. Videodiscs and the hardware to play them are among the oldest and most stable technologies available for multimedia. A videodisc is a 12-inch shiny silver disc that contains analog audio and video information embedded into it by a laser. The videodisc can hold thirty minutes of high-quality full-motion video and sixty minutes of audio per side. Some or all of the motion video can be replaced by up to 54,000 still images per videodisc side.

The videodisc player can randomly access any portion of the motion video or audio, or any of the 54,000 still images within a few seconds. The speed of access depends on the characteristics of the player. The videodisc player can be controlled by a hand-held key pad, a laser bar code reader, or a computer. The keypad is somewhat awkward to use, thereby limiting interactivity, and is not discussed further. The bar code reader is used by scanning a bar code on a sheet of paper and then activating the player. The nature of the bar code determines which video, stills, and audio the player presents. A computer connects to a videodisc player via an industry standard RS-232C serial cable in most cases, or possibly through a serial port. The computer is programmed to allow the user to select the audio and video information contained on the videodisc.

Computer-controlled interactive videodisc systems usually come in two types. The first type, known as a two-screen system, is usually less expensive and consists of a videodisc player, a computer with a monitor, and a separate audio/video monitor. The computer screen shows any computer-generated information, such as text and graphics, and the audiovisual screen provides any videodisc information, such as video or audio. The second type of system uses an interface card,

Interactive Media Characteristics

	Analog/ Digital	Storage Medium	Media Size	Platforms	Motion Video	Audio	Stills	Graphics overlay	Video manipulation	Video format	Audio/Video editing
DVI	Digital	CD-ROM, hard disk, other digital devices	5-1/4" CD-ROMs, hard disks	AT and clones, PS-2, Macintosh	72 min. full-screen, full-motion	Up to 40 hours, up to 2 output channels	Up to 40,000 max res. of 1024 x 512	Yes	High speed, hardware-accelerated software driven	Compressed	Yes
CD-I	Digital	CD-ROM	5-1/4" CD-ROMs integrated	Integrated consumer player	72 min. full-screen, full motion	Up to 19 hours, up to 2 output channels	Up to 8,000, max. res. of 720 x 480	Yes	Lower speed, hardware supported	Compressed	Yes
IVD	Analog	Videodisc player	12" discs	Several incompatible systems, interfaced to a variety of computers	30 min./side	30 min./side 2 channels	54,000 per side about 640 x 480 res.	Requires computer add-in board	Additional hardware required	Standard	No
CD-XA	Digital	CD-ROM	5-1/4" CD-ROMs	Computers with SCSI interface	NA	Up to 19 hours, up to 2 output channels	NA	Yes	NA	NA	Yes
CDTV	Digital	CD-ROM	5-1/4" CD-ROMs	Integrated consumer player	NA	NA 2 output channels	NA	Yes	NA	Compressed	Yes
LD-ROM	Both	Videodisc player	12" discs	System interfaced to a variety of computers	30 min./side	30 min./side 2 channels	54,000 per side,* about 640 x 480 res.	Requires computer add-in board	Additional hardware required	Standard	Yes

NA: Information not available
*: Disc also includes 270 MB of digital data

Table 4.1 (Galbreath, 1992a)

allowing it to present on a single screen both the video information from the videodisc and text and graphics from the computer.

Three levels of videodisc applications are available. Level One is the least automated—the user controls the player manually using a hand controller or a bar code reader, much like the operation of a VCR. Level Two is characterized by a videodisc player with an internal microprocessor that can read a computer program encoded into the videodisc at the time of manufacture. Level Three videodisc applications involve a videodisc player controlled by an external computer. In this case the videodisc player is a peripheral device to the computer, which controls all of the player's operations.

Videodiscs can be formatted in two different ways. A CAV (constant angular velocity) videodisc can have thirty minutes of running video per side, and each of the 54,000 frames per side can be individually addressed and displayed. A CLV (constant linear velocity) or extended play videodisc can have up to sixty minutes of video per side, but individual frames are not addressable. CLV videodiscs can be addressed and played by time and chapter.

As suggested above, interactive videodiscs contain information encoded in an analog format. Increasingly, however, newer technologies employ a digital format. The analog format involves a series of pits in the videodisc created during the manufacturing process by a laser and subsequently "read" by a laser in the videodisc player. The advantages of analog information include high-quality video and a dense and accessible storage medium; a disadvantage is that the user cannot alter the information encoded on the disc. The digital formats described below reduce all video and audio to a series of "1"s and "0"s, much as a computer now encodes text and graphics. The advantages of the digital approach include the ability to readily alter the information; the disadvantages include the large amounts of computer memory needed to store video images.

CD-ROM. CD-ROM was introduced in 1985 as a medium for the mass storage of computer-readable text. Each 4.72-inch disc stores approximately 650 megabytes (MB) of digital data. CD-ROM discs can store digital text, graphics, audio, and video images. Because of its large storage capacity, CD-ROM is often used for storage and retrieval of large bodies of information such as extended databases and encyclopedias.

Despite its storage capabilities, CD-ROM use has been limited as a multimedia source by the immense storage requirements of high-quality, full-motion video. These limitations are being addressed by the platforms described below.

Digital video interactive. Motion video takes huge quantities of memory in its original digitized form; therefore, the digital information must be compressed for a multimedia application. DVI (digital video interactive) is based on a set of compression algorithms designed to overcome the major problems of digital video storage. The reduction enables application developers to include up to an hour of full-motion video on a single storage device, such as a CD-ROM or a hard disk.

DVI consists of add-in cards for both capture and delivery. These cards are installed in the computer and can convert either an Apple Macintosh or an IBM PC to a fully functional DVI system. The capture board can convert audio or video from any NTSC (United States standard television) input to digital data and is required for those wishing to develop their own DVI applications. The delivery board compresses and decompresses full-motion, full-screen video in real time and allows viewing of off-the-shelf applications or of applications developed with the capture board.

Compact disc-interactive. CD-I provides the capability of storing digital color images, text, graphics, audio, applications software, and compressed full-motion video on a CD-ROM. Developed jointly by Phillips and Sony, CD-I consists of a standalone unit that both reads the compact disc and performs the functions of a computer. Developed ultimately for the home consumer market, CD-I systems come equipped with a mouse or a remote control unit much like a VCR and operate much like a video game.

CD-I has already developed standards that enable any CD-I or CD audio disc to play on any CD-I player in the world. Applications are increasingly becoming available, and CD-I is emerging as an affordable and highly interactive multimedia delivery system.

CD-ROM extended architecture. CD-ROM/XA is a computer peripheral device that adds digital audio and graphics to CD-ROM data. A drive is required to read the audio portions of the disc, and an audio card in the computer is added to transform the digital data into sound. Microsoft and its development partners have demonstrated that CD-ROM/XA can provide limited amounts of motion video, and this capability is likely to be expanded in the future.

Other platforms Pioneer has developed laserdisc read-only memory (LD-ROM), which combines on a single 12-inch disc the thirty minutes of full-motion video and stereo sound of an analog videodisc with the 270 megabytes of digitized computer data of a CD-ROM. LD-ROM currently bridges the gap between the laserdisc and the newer digital technologies, and efforts are already underway to convert the analog portions of this platform to store the data digitally.

Commodore Dynamic Total Vision (CDTV) is similar to CD-I as a digital-based, standalone unit aimed primarily at the consumer market. It combines Amiga's graphics, video, and sound chips into a complete unit that also incorporates interactive text, graphics, video, stills, and animation of a CD-ROM. As with LD-ROM, it remains to be seen whether a sufficient application base to support the expansion of this hardware will develop.

Components of Multimedia Systems

Key elements of multimedia platforms include computers, videodisc players, CD-ROM drives, devices for inputting information, and devices for outputting or presenting information. Each of these key elements is described below, followed by some observations on the current trends related to multimedia hardware.

Computers. Computers form the core of most multimedia development and delivery systems. Because Apple Macintosh and IBM and compatible computers constitute the overwhelming choice of people in higher education, it is reasonable to believe that these computers will support the multimedia systems that are ultimately the standard in colleges and universities. Each of these families of computers, along with their multimedia capabilities, is described below.

Macintosh computers have numerous capabilities suitable for use with multimedia. They generally provide high-speed processors, easy access to digitized sound and video, and simple connections to various peripheral devices. Macintosh's ease of use and large base of third-party hardware and software are additional advantages. Different Macintosh models provide a balance between price and performance features and options.

For a basic two-screen delivery system, the Macintosh Classic II, Macintosh LC III, or Macintosh 575 will support a videodisc player or CD-ROM drive for about $1,000. Several off-the-shelf CD-ROM applications, such as *Martin Luther King* and others from ABC Interactive, and CD-audio applications of classic music from Voyager and Warner New Media can be delivered effectively with these Macintosh computers. Two-screen videodisc applications can be readily programmed using HyperCard or some other straightforward programming tool. QuickTime can also be used on these models, but digital video lacks options available with higher priced models.

Older, middle-range models, such as the Macintosh IIci or Macintosh IIvx, offer more speed and flexibility than their lower priced counterparts. These options allow single screen and two-screen delivery and development capabilities with appropriate cards and/or peripheral devices. Greater processing speed and additional slots provide multimedia systems based on the greater flexibility and growth options for these models.

Newer Macintosh Quadra models offer significantly enhanced capability, speed, and flexibility. These models have speedy processors, fast connections for cards and peripheral devices, and built-in support for 24-bit color. The Quadra 610 and 840 AV models have built-in audiovisual capabilities and are designed for multimedia use.

The Power Mac series of computers offers the advantages of evolving RISC (reduced instruction set computer) technology and built-in audio and visual capabilities. The Power Mac 6100, 7100, and 8100 all offer AV models and built-in CD-ROM drives, making digital multimedia accessible in a single package in the $2,500 to $5,000 range. The Macintosh PowerBook series offers the advantage of portability for those who want to bring multimedia into the classroom. The PowerBook 145 and 165 models support an external monitor and color with a weight of only about seven pounds. The PowerBook 520 and 520c models have passive matrix screens that limit their capability to display digital applications. The PowerBook 540 and 540c models have an active matrix screen that facilitates digital multimedia display. All PowerBooks can be used effectively with two-screen systems. Many multimedia capabilities of larger Macs are being integrated into the PowerBook series.

The IBM family and compatibles also offer a range of alternatives, ranging from the PC and compatible to the PS/2 to the Ultimedia system. The PC market has not always incorporated the multimedia capabilities of Macintosh, but offers considerable flexibility with add-ons and has developed integrated systems with significant capabilities. Various options are described briefly below.

The basic PC and compatibles can still be used for relatively straightforward applications. With appropriate cards and graphics capabilities, almost any DOS-based PC can function as the central component of either a two-screen or basic one-screen system that incorporates a videodisc player, CD-ROM, or other peripheral device. More sophisticated applications and uses require a 80486 or more advanced processor. Because many of the components of these PC-based systems were designed individually, getting them to work together can be challenging.

The plethora of potential PC multimedia platforms, and their resulting incompatibilities, have led to an emerging standard for PC-based multimedia. To address this problem, a number of vendors joined together to create the Multimedia PC (MPC) Marketing Council. This group set the minimum standard for equipment to run a common set of multimedia applications (Miller, 1992). The first standard for an MPC machine required, among other things, an 80386SX processor or better, a CD-ROM fast enough to run multimedia titles, support for MIDI and waveform audio, and Microsoft Windows with Multimedia Extensions 1.0, better known as Multimedia Extensions. A system meeting these standards can be purchased for about $1,400 and upgrade kits are available for less than $500. This standard has been upgraded to MPC 2 and will likely be further upgraded in the future.

IBM and compatible computers continue to provide advances in speed and flexibility required for digital-based multimedia. The Intel 80386 chip was replaced by the superior speed of the 80486 chip, and the Pentium PC now offers 66 MHz speed and expandability that will facilitate a remarkable set of multimedia capabilities with added cards and peripherals (see below). Over a dozen vendors now offer Pentium PC computers.

IBM's Ultimedia system represents an alternative standard. It allows use of some of the most sophisticated multimedia applications currently available and supports a variety of development activities. This system allows easy integration of videodisc- and CD-ROM-based data and has an increasing set of applications available.

Both PC and Macintosh systems are moving toward digital-based applications and efforts are being made to develop standards so that applications can be used on hardware from different vendors. The Macintosh has historically integrated more multimedia capabilities with each computer unit and can therefore readily plug into a variety of peripheral devices without adding extra cards. PCs have a variety of capabilities that can be incorporated through cards, and standards are being developed between machines to provide compatibility.

Videodisc players. There are probably more videodisc applications appropriate for use in higher education than any other type of multimedia application, making the inclusion of a videodisc player essential in most multimedia delivery systems. Pioneer dominates the industrial videodisc player market; its current line of players most appropriate for college and university settings are described below.

The Pioneer CLD-V2400 player can play 8-inch and 12-inch videodiscs, CDs, CD singles, and CDV discs. It is bar code compatible or can be connected to a computer with an RS-232C interface. It has text overlay capabilities and a maximum search time to a specific frame of five seconds in the CAV format. The Pioneer CLD-V2400 player costs about $800.

The Pioneer LD-V4400 videodisc player accommodates only videodiscs, but has an average search time of only one second with the CAV format. It is also bar code compatible or can use the standard RS-232C interface with the computer. This player can provide text overlay and four-channel audio, with two digital channels and two analog channels. The Pioneer LD-V4400 costs about $1,100.

The Pioneer LD-V8000 videodisc player has many of the same features as the LD-V4400 but with several enhancements. The LD-V8000 can play Level Two videodiscs in both CAV and CLV. It has very rapid search speed (maximum 0.5 seconds with CAV format). This player has digital video memory, so it can provide for seamless search without video loss and can display a still image while at the same time providing random access audio. The LD-V8000 costs about $2,000.

Sony also manufactures a line of videodisc players. The Sony line includes players with features and costs similar to the Pioneer CLD-V2400 and LD-V4400. At this time Sony offers no player comparable to the Pioneer LD-V8000.

CD-ROM drives. The number of CD-ROM titles is increasing rapidly, making a CD-ROM drive an essential component in multimedia delivery systems. CD-ROM applications are typically used to store large amounts of text and graphic information and are increasingly used as a means of storing still pictures, video, and audio. The prices of these drives have come down and now sell in the $200 to $500 range, depending on the features included.

One of the key capabilities to consider in a CD-ROM drive is the speed, both in terms of access time and data transfer rate. *Access time*, measured in milliseconds, is the average time required for the drive to locate a random piece of information. It defines the critical performance measure for repeated searches in a large database to pull out small bits of information. *Transfer rate*, measured in kilobytes per second, indicates the time it takes a drive to transfer information to a computer's central processing unit (CPU). Transfer rate matters most to those using multimedia titles, because finding data is secondary to transferring it rapidly and smoothly to the CPU for display. Double-speed is currently a minimum standard.

A number of manufacturers produce CD-ROM drives, including Apple, NEC, Sony, and Panasonic among the larger corporations. Smaller companies include CD Technology, Optical Access International, and Mirror Technologies. Key considerations in choosing among drives from these and other companies include access speed, transfer rate, the software and applications bundled with the drive, and features such as being able to read Kodak's Photo CD, which allows film to be developed onto a CD and subsequently displayed with a drive and possibly a computer. Multi-session drives are important in using Photo CD.

Devices for inputting information. When developing or repurposing multimedia applications, a number of devices can be incorporated to increase the range of elements that can be integrated into these applications. There are a number of ways to get video and images into a computer; this section focuses on external devices that can input sources of video.

Scanners can import pictures into a computer for use in multimedia applications. Scanners range from low-cost, hand-held devices that can "copy" small black and white pictures to sophisticated flatbed color scanners that can import high-resolution color images. Apple, Logitech, Panasonic, and Sony are among the manufacturers of these convenient and powerful tools for inputting images into a computer for multimedia use.

Recently developed still video (SV) technology gets higher resolution "photographs" into a computer by going directly from the camera to the machine. Digital SV cameras link directly to a computer, and analog SV cameras require a digitizing board in the computer. Both types enable educators to take pictures of anything, anywhere—just as you would with a regular camera. Canon, Apple, and Logitech are three of the companies marketing SV cameras.

Camcorders are versatile tools that can be used to input motion video for use with multimedia. A number of different types exist, ranging from the low-resolution S-VHS format that might also be used to capture family reunions to extremely high-resolution CCD cameras. The type of camcorder selected must match the intended use. For import into a computer, a video digitizing card or special external video/computer interface box is required. Canon, Panasonic, Sharp, Sony, and Toshiba are among the companies providing camcorders.

Devices for presenting or outputting information. Delivery systems require an effective means of presenting multimedia-based information to students. The devices required depend on the situation in which multimedia instruction will be used. When students are using multimedia as individuals or in small groups as a learning tool, the computer screen itself and sometimes a standard video monitor will suffice, but presentations to larger groups require more sophisticated and therefore more expensive devices.

The easiest way to provide multimedia instruction for a larger group is simply to use a larger monitor. Large-screen monitors can be readily viewed by up to thirty to fifty students, depending on the type of video being displayed, and represent a straightforward way of involving more students in multimedia instruction.

LCD (liquid crystal display) panels act as conduits between computers and overhead projectors, performing in a sense like electronic transparencies. Until recently, most panels displayed in monochrome, but newer technology allows panels to display thousands of colors at VGA resolutions. Most standard monochrome and color panels can display animation and simulations, but not motion video, although recent innovations have also provided full-motion display capability on more expensive panels. Active matrix screens are essential in displaying digital video. Sharp, nVIEW, and In Focus are among the companies marketing LCD panels.

Video/data projectors can project text, graphics, animations, photos, and motion video, and in color, if desired. The three categories of projectors involve light valves, LCD, and cathode ray tube (CRT) construction. Each of these types has advantages and disadvantages, which are beyond the scope of this section to examine. These projectors provide excellent opportunities for presenting multimedia applications to large groups.

Output devices offer one capability that monitors, LCD panels, and projectors do not—they provide a permanent printed copy for each student. Standard printers can provide copies of text and graphics, but color, as a mainstay of multimedia, is lost. Color printers can print computer screens, and video printers can generate hard copy from a video-based source. Canon and Sony are among the companies marketing these devices.

Add-in cards. A number of different integral functions are made possible by add-in cards, all related to sound and video capabilities. Sound capabilities include stereo audio and MIDI for connecting instruments, the ability to record voice and sound effects via a microphone, and a stereo mixer for combining analog and digital audio. Video capabilities include frame grabbers for capturing and digitizing single frames of motion video; genlock, to synchronize an incoming video signal to the computer; graphics overlay; conversion of television signals (NTSC in the United States and PAL and SECAM in much of the rest of the world) so that they can be displayed on a computer screen; real-time video compression for storage; and decompression for full-motion playback.

These cards are complicated. Some computers (such as more recent and powerful Macintoshes) have significant audio and video capabilities built in; other computers require cards for most multimedia functions. Some cards provide only sound capabilities, some do only video, and others provide both. Reviews of various cards and their capabilities are included in periodicals for PCs, Macs, and other computers (see "Resources" section of this chapter).

A number of vendors make add-in cards. IBM markets M-Audio and M-Motion cards for PC-DOS, PS/1, and PS/2 computers. Farallon, Radius, RasterOps, and SuperMac are leading vendors for Macintosh cards. VideoLogic, IEV, and New Media Graphics are among other card vendors.

Mass storage systems. Multimedia requires huge amounts of memory for digital applications; fortunately a variety of mass storage options exist. Hard disks offer increasingly large capacities and are decreasing in price per storage unit. Removable media systems are basically a hard disk in a cartridge, with capacity limited only by the number of 44-MB, 88-MB, or 200-MB cartridges that one can afford. Optical disk drives have capacities up to one gigabyte (1,000 megabytes), but are slower than standard hard disks or removable media systems. Very high density (VHD) and floptical drives are increasingly viable storage options. Numerous vendors are marketing mass storage devices.

Integrated systems. Computers, videodisc players, CD-ROM drives, and other components of a multimedia system, when selected separately, make it difficult to mix and match the various devices effectively and to obtain and install the appropriate cables, software, and connectors to make the platform functional. Integrated systems avoid some of these difficulties. IBM's InfoWindow and Sony's View systems are earlier examples of integrated systems; MPC and IBM's Ultimedia are current examples.

Current trends related to multimedia hardware. Videodisc platforms were among the earliest multimedia devices and have been the most stable for some years, resulting in a large number of available applications. CD-ROM has been used as a storage device for large amounts of data for some time, and therefore a number of those applications also are available. Digital video has become more available recently, and standards are emerging, leading to a rapid increase in CD-based applications that can be transferable from one platform to another.

The unmistakable trend is toward digital-based multimedia. QuickTime on the Macintosh and DVI for PCs are making digital full-motion video, the core capability of multimedia, more widely available. Nonetheless, the number of videodisc applications, the established player base, and the image quality of videodiscs will likely keep videodisc platforms viable in higher education for the foreseeable future.

Questions

1. What are the educational problems and goals that you will attempt to address using multimedia? (See Chapter 3.)
2. How might you use multimedia—as a teaching tool, a learning tool, or both? (See Chapter 5.)
3. What multimedia applications are either available or could be developed to address these educational problems and goals? (See Chapters 6 to 8.)
4. What types of multimedia hardware systems and components will be required to develop and use these applications?
5. What types of multimedia systems are currently available on campus (Interactive Video, CD-ROM DVI, other systems)?
6. What components of multimedia systems are currently available to you (computers, videodisc players, CD-ROM drives, input devices, output devices, mass storage devices, integrated systems)?

7. What additional multimedia systems and components could become available to my campus and to me in the near future?
8. What are sources of funds to obtain multimedia hardware?

Examples

As in other chapters, the authors' experiences provide some concrete examples of issues surrounding multimedia hardware. At the University of Minnesota, Duluth, there are pockets of interest among faculty in various disciplines in which educational problems that could be addressed by multimedia have been defined. The campus does possess a variety of multimedia systems and components, many of which are available for faculty use in instruction. Examples from three disciplinary areas are provided, focusing on educational problems and goals, potential multimedia applications, and hardware considerations.

Educational Problems and Goals

Teacher education faculty have a number of goals for students, including development of excellent communication skills, an understanding of group dynamics, and a sensitivity to issues related to human diversity. Art history teachers want students to learn to examine works critically from a variety of artists over many historical eras, and music appreciation instructors want students to learn to understand prominent works from a variety of perspectives. Biology teachers want students to examine visual examples of a number of different biological concepts and processes, and chemistry teachers want large numbers of students to have specific laboratory experiences.

Potential Multimedia Applications

Several applications that could address the problems and goals described above are either currently available on the University of Minnesota, Duluth campus or could be obtained at a relatively low cost. With regard to teacher education, one application was developed on campus to help students understand Southeast Asian refugees, and the *Martin Luther King, Jr* application developed by ABC Interactive is available in the library's audio-visual department. The former requires an IBM InfoWindow system, and the latter can be used on a Macintosh computer with any one of a number of videodisc players.

Applications are also available to achieve goals related to the fine arts. The University of Minnesota, Duluth owns videodisc applications that include collections of the Louvre Museum in Paris and the National Gallery of Art in Washington, D. C. Numerous other videodiscs are available for other artists or galleries. The two currently available videodisc applications in art require a Macintosh and videodisc player. In music, the multimedia application on *The Magic Flute* from Warner New Media is currently available, and *The Rite of Spring* or *Beethoven's Ninth Symphony* could each be available from the Voyager Company for less than $100. These music applications require a Macintosh or PC and a CD-ROM drive.

Science needs can also be addressed by multimedia applications, although none are currently available on campus. Examples of biological concepts and processes can be provided in the classroom either by obtaining the *BioSci II* application for about $600 or perhaps by obtaining a generic biology videodisc free from a publisher and repurposing it for use in a particular course. Either PCs or a Macintosh could be used for this purpose. *Doing Chemistry* is an example of an application that can provide numerous simulated laboratory demonstrations and experiments using a Macintosh and any RS-232C videodisc player, and this application can be obtained from the American Chemical Society for about $600.

Hardware Considerations

Some of the foregoing educational problems and goals could be addressed by using available applications on existing equipment. In the short term, additional equipment could be added to more fully meet the existing educational goals. In the long term, additional considerations will need to be addressed. Examples of each of these possibilities are provided below.

Using existing hardware. The University of Minnesota, Duluth owns a variety of equipment that either has been or could be used to provide multimedia instruction. A Macintosh-based system with a Pioneer 8000 videodisc player and CD-ROM drive and an IBM Ultimedia system are on carts that can be wheeled into about 95 percent of the classrooms on campus. Because both these systems have appropriate presentation devices available, they can be used for very small classes as well as for classes with up to 300 students. The university also has two IBM InfoWindow systems and one system including a Macintosh SE, a Pioneer 2200 videodisc player, a CD-ROM drive, and headphones. These three systems are stationary in a lab and are designed for individual or small group use outside the classroom.

In a teacher education class on human diversity, the instructor could use the *Martin Luther King, Jr.* application in the classroom to demonstrate aspects of Dr. King's philosophy of nonviolence, to share significant events in the Civil Rights Movement, and to see and hear significant portions of the "I have a dream" speech, all by presenting selected portions of the video and audio from the application. This application could use the mobile Macintosh system described above. The two InfoWindow systems in the lab could be used for students to interact individually or in pairs with the application on Southeast Asian refugees, finding out more about different cultures, potential difficulties for refugee children in schools, and what teachers can do to better meet the refugee students' needs.

The same mobile Macintosh systems could be scheduled for use in the classroom by the music appreciation instructor or the biology instructor. The music instructor could use the Magic Flute application and hook the Macintosh system into the large classroom's existing sound system to examine various aspects of this classic Mozart work. The biology instructor could hook the system up to a large screen presentation device from the campus audio-visual center to share visual examples of key concepts and processes in an introductory biology course with up to 250 students.

Short-term hardware considerations. In some cases the existing hardware is not sufficient to meet the educational goals in a particular area. For example, if the instructor wanted each of the 200 students in an introductory chemistry class to experience ten demonstrations or experiments from the *Doing Chemistry* application during a particular quarter, the single Macintosh systems currently available would certainly be insufficient to meet student demand in the lab. If each experiment/demonstration took about an hour and could be done in pairs, about three additional Macintosh-based systems would be required to schedule students' access to the applications relatively easily. An approximate cost of $10,000 for the additional systems ($2,400 for each of the three low-end Macintosh Classic systems with a videodisc player and a monitor, and $600 for each of the three additional copies of the *Doing Chemistry* application) would be relatively high, but in the long run would probably be more cost effective than maintaining and updating chemistry laboratories and paying laboratory assistants.

Long-term hardware considerations. It may be more cost effective in the long run to purchase hardware that will be more versatile in responding to future trends in multimedia. If one considered these trends when purchasing the three Macintosh systems described above, a Power Mac 6100 AV might be a better computer at the core of the systems. Although not required for the current application, this computer would offer much more flexibility in the future because more and more applications will be digital-based.

Guidelines

Several guidelines provide information for understanding and obtaining multimedia hardware.

1. Before exploring multimedia hardware options, have a clear understanding of the educational goals and problems you will be addressing.
2. Hardware should be examined in conjunction with the applications that are available for use with a particular configuration.
3. In general, it is better to start simple. Using one low-end system as an instructional tool in the classroom will help clarify the advantages and limitations of multimedia.
4. See what equipment is currently available on your campus; you may be surprised to discover that a variety of hardware is already available and ready to use.
5. Determine whether you need a delivery system or a development system. Delivery systems are generally less expensive, but development systems are more flexible and are required if you are going to develop applications, particularly of the digital-based applications.

6. Carefully examine the hardware required to meet defined education goals with specific applications, and obtain hardware that is necessary to meet that need in the short term.
7. In the long term it may be better to coordinate with other campus users and seek a multimedia laboratory that will not only meet current and short-term needs, but long-term needs as well.
8. The future of multimedia is digital.

Resources

A variety of resources, both on your local campus and beyond, can be of value in learning about and obtaining multimedia equipment.

Campus Colleagues

Other faculty members and staff in various units around the campus can be a key resource for learning about multimedia hardware. The computer center staff will often know about those capabilities centered in the computer, such as digital video, graphics, animation, and control of peripherals. Staff in the campus audio-visual center are more likely to know about videodisc and CD-ROM applications. Library staff members are increasingly knowledgeable about CD-ROM and their use as databases. Several members of the faculty on your campus may have knowledge and experience with multimedia hardware and may be happy to share their expertise with potential supporters. Be aware that these individuals may only know of multimedia from their own perspectives and that a balanced view is important.

Conferences

One of the most efficient, but more expensive, ways of learning about multimedia hardware is to attend conferences in which multimedia is a significant part of the exhibit section. Examples of conferences in which multimedia hardware is likely to be prominent include SALT, COMDEX, Intermedia, and Multimedia Expo. Other multimedia-oriented conferences are listed in the resource section of the appendix.

Vendors

Hardware suppliers are an excellent source of current information on the multimedia hardware available. These vendors often have 800 numbers and will send out information after receiving an inquiry by telephone, fax, e-mail or mail. National numbers in the United States and United Kingdom are listed in the appendix. Additionally, the computer center or bookstore on your campus or local resellers may know vendors' campus representatives who can provide direct information about hardware options.

Computer and Multimedia Periodicals

Periodicals associated with various computers often include basic information and reviews of multimedia hardware. *MacUser* and *MacWorld* are examples for

Apple users; *PC Magazine* and *PC World* are examples for IBM and compatible users. *New Media, The World of Macintosh Multimedia, Multimedia World,* and *T.H.E Journal*, particularly in its annual *Multimedia Source Guide*, provide information about all types of multimedia hardware.

Conclusion

Computer technology makes possible all of the remarkable learning and teaching capabilities associated with multimedia; and the equipment is also the most complex and dynamic topic related to using multimedia in higher education. It is important that you have a basic understanding of what the hardware can do, experience it first hand whenever possible, and know what the market offers when you get to the point of actually purchasing equipment. Above all, it is important to keep in mind the educational problems and goals you want to address and to focus on the potential benefits of multimedia, discounting the puffery sounded by the vendors. It is also vital that you examine the hardware in the context of the multimedia applications that are available or could be developed, and the type of use to which these applications will be put. The next four chapters examine these topics.

CHAPTER 5

GENERATING SOLUTIONS: METHODS AND MODELS FOR USING MULTIMEDIA

Goals

Multimedia hardware provides marvelous capabilities for enhancing teaching and learning. Before actually using its capabilities, one should devise a framework for combining multimedia elements, such as video, audio, text, graphics, and animation, into coherent applications that can then be used to facilitate teaching and learning. One must also be familiar with optional methods for actually using applications for teaching and learning.

This chapter focuses on five models of instruction that can be incorporated into applications and on two methods for use of hardware and applications that are enhanced by multimedia; it further describes how these methods of use and models of instruction relate to one another. The chapter also includes some background information on multimedia design and specific examples of models of instruction and methods of use.

General Information

Instructional Design Models

The capabilities and flexibility of multimedia make this technology an ideal vehicle for including a wide variety of instructional models, and numerous authors have described instructional models that take advantage of multimedia's varied capabilities. Floyd and Floyd (1982) emphasize the importance of thinking interactively when designing multimedia instruction. Wlodkowski (1989) emphasizes the central issue of learner motivation in instructional design. Daynes (1987) provides over twenty models of instruction made possible with multimedia. Iuppa (1990) and Iuppa and Anderson (1988) provide a number of examples of lesson design offering various degrees of learner choices.

This chapter focuses on five generic instructional models that have proven effective for multimedia applications (Falk & Carlson, 1991; Falk & Carlson, 1992). These five models are described in general terms in the section below, with examples provided from multimedia applications that are currently available. Specific cases of how each of these models have been used at the authors' institution appear in the "Examples" section.

Video-enhanced didactic presentations. This instruction model often takes the form of a well-organized lecture/presentation that selectively uses text, audio, graphics, and video to present content in a direct and straightforward manner. Concepts and information can come alive with the incorporation of video and other multimedia capabilities.

One example of this instructional model is *Atoms to Anatomy: A Multimedia View of Human Systems*, published by Videodiscovery. This multimedia application allows an anatomy instructor to augment a didactic presentation with videodisc-based color stills and video of skeletal and muscular structures, the central nervous system, cardiology, respiration, and circulation. It also includes animation and three-dimensional models of selected organs, tissues, cells, and molecules that can be tilted and rotated for students to view.

Exploration. Models involving exploration allow learners to move through a multimedia application individually and to explore a variety of information that is available in text, graphics, video, and audio formats. Categories of information are often linked to one another through the use of hypertext or icons that move the learner throughout the application, enabling a relatively free flowing discovery of the application's contents. Learners are sometimes partially guided through an application or can explore the application completely through their own choices.

The Magic Flute application from Warner New Media allows a student to explore Mozart's operatic masterwork in a variety of ways. The student can select any portion of the opera for listening, follow the plot or orchestration with text information that is synchronized to the music, see the lyrics in either English or German as they are sung, and obtain background information on Mozart's life and times in text and graphics. In this case the instructor could guide the students toward particular portions of the opera or content in the analysis, or let the students work completely on their own.

Structured observation. This instructional model refers to learners following set guidelines in observing video segments or another aspect of a multimedia application. Often the application or the instructor focus students' attention on a particular aspect of a phenomenon they will view, and the students make observations and then receive feedback on the specific observations they could have made. Video examples can be viewed repeatedly, even in slow motion, if desired.

The *Living Textbook—Physical Science* provides ample opportunity for structured observation using 2,500 still images and 90 video clips to cover basic concepts in matter, motion, forces, waves, electricity, and magnetism. Learners can be introduced to specific concepts, watch a clip of an example of the concept, and then hear about what they have seen.

Simulated personal interaction. This instructional model involves creating a case study or situation in which learners participate, and influence interaction, in the multimedia application. Learners are encouraged to become a part of an interaction, with the persons in the application seemingly speaking with them and the actions that the learner chooses affecting the nature of the interaction.

Decision Point, an earlier videodisc-based application developed by the Digital Equipment Company, made effective use of simulated personal interaction. The learner was hired as a new manager of sales and then allowed to collect information about a number of situations related to the new job by talking with colleagues; the learner then made choices that affected the outcome of sales and staff morale. Throughout the application the learner's colleagues talk directly with the learner and seek the learner's input in various ways.

Assessment and focused instruction This instructional model involves testing a learner's knowledge of a particular topic and then directing the student to an appropriate level of instruction or remediation. The testing can take the form of a pretest that then places the learner into the proper level of instruction; the testing can also be undertaken after initial instruction to determine whether any remediation is necessary.

An example of an application using this model of instruction is *Interactive ModuMath*, which provides self-paced, individualized, competency-based instruction in basic math and algebra. The application includes a computer-based placement test, randomly generated lesson tests, and comprehensive record keeping abilities. The videodisc-based lessons provide instruction that is visual and precise.

Combinations of instructional models. Many multimedia applications include more than one of these instructional design models. Additionally, these designs sometimes merge. The design models described above do provide ways of thinking about the kinds of instruction that are enhanced through multimedia. One of the advantages of multimedia is that using these tools can open a teacher's views of innovative models of instruction that are available, thereby expanding the options available to meet a particular student's or group's educational needs.

Methods for Using Multimedia Applications

In the broadest sense, the use of multimedia applications can fall into two categories: as a teaching tool and as a learning tool. Definitions and examples of each of these types of uses, and the differences between them, are described below.

Teaching tool. Model T, using the application as a teaching tool, involves the instructor selectively using specific aspects of an application to enhance her or his presentation or coverage of a particular topic in the context of a class meeting. In using multimedia as a teaching tool, instructors can integrate computer text and graphics, video, still images, and audio to develop classroom presentations that are stimulating, interactive, informative, and flexible.

Several of the applications mentioned as examples of instructional models above can be used as teaching tools. An instructor could use the *Atoms to Anatomy* application with a large-screen projector to provide video and graphic examples of key anatomical systems and structures in an anatomy course. *Decision Point* could be used as a case study in a classroom, with the instructor stopping the application at various points to discuss with the students optional actions that could be taken. *The Magic Flute* could be used by a music instructor in a classroom context to explore several aspects of a particular movement in the score or scene of the opera.

Learning tool. Model L, using the application as a learning tool, involves the learner interacting with the instructional program in a self-directed manner. Multimedia applications can incorporate all of the features described above into a learning tool that provides individualized, self-paced, interactive instruction outside of the classroom. This instruction can incorporate multimedia as an *individualized learning tool* (Model LI) if only one student interacts with the application or as a *small-group learning tool* (Model LG) if two or more students interact with the application simultaneously.

Several of the applications used as examples of instructional models could also be used as learning tools outside the classroom. *The Magic Flute* could be used by students to explore various aspects of that opera in an individualized and self-directed way, either in preparation for studying the work in class or as an enrichment after the work was introduced. Students could use *The Living Textbook-Physical Sciences* application in a learning center to conduct simulated experiments in pairs, much as they would do in a physics lab. The *Interactive ModuMath* applications could provide assessment and focused instruction to individual learners requiring remediation in an algebra course.

Differences in the methods. Key differences in these two methods of using multimedia are apparent. The teaching tool method, as its name indicates, is teacher directed. The learning tool method is curriculum-driven in that the learner makes choices offered by the application's computer program. Model L offers individualized, self-paced instruction that can accommodate different learning styles, while Model T is more flexible, because the instructor is present and can alter the curriculum based on student response. Model L requires more equipment and sometimes more supervision if many students are to use an application over a period of time; Model T requires the means to project a computer screen and/or video images so that they are clearly visible to everyone in a class. While a key component of both methods is interactivity, the teaching method allows the teacher to control the nature of the interactivity more directly.

One of the best ways to understand these two uses of multimedia and the differences between them is to consider the other teaching tools that can be replaced or enhanced by multimedia. As a teaching tool, multimedia can become an electronic blackboard or overhead projector that incorporates text, graphics, and animation; a slide projector with 54,000 slides in the carousel, each of which can be accessed in less than five seconds; a VCR with thirty minutes of video that can be randomly accessed in seconds; and a stereophonic audiotape player, which can also be accessed quickly and randomly. As a learning tool, multimedia can be thought of as a book that incorporates sound, animation, and video; a lab station that can simulate hundreds of experiments; or computer-based instruction that includes sound and video.

An Integrated Model for Instructional Design and Use

Each of the five instructional design models described above can be applied by using the applications as either a teaching tool in a classroom or as a learning tool with individuals or small groups. Figure 5-1 presents an integrated model for the design and use of multimedia in teaching and learning settings. The integrated model presented in this figure suggests that an application incorporating any of the instructional models described above could be used as either a teaching or a learning tool, although some models are more suited for one or the other. The examples described above are included in the matrix.

Instructional Design Model					
Method of Use	Didactic Presentation	Exploration	Structured Observation	Simulated Interaction	Assessment & Instruction
Model T Teaching Tool	Atoms to Anatomy	The Magic Flute		Decision Point	
Model L Learning Tool		The Magic Flute	The Living Textbook— Physical Science		Interactive ModuMath

Figure 5.1   **An Integrated Model for Instructional Design and Use**

Questions

1. How could different models of instruction be used to take advantage of multimedia's capabilities to achieve defined educational goals? Video-enhanced didactic presentations? Exploration? Structured observation? Simulated personal interaction? Assessment and focused instruction?
2. How could multimedia be used as a teaching tool to enhance classroom instruction?
3. How could multimedia be used as a teaching tool to enhance instruction outside of the classroom?

4. How could the methods and models of instruction identified above be integrated with multimedia hardware to provide effective instruction to address particular educational problems on my campus?

Examples

Over a four-year period, the College of Education and Human Service Professions produced eight multimedia applications centered around the use of videodiscs. Background on the nature of these applications is described below. They provide concrete examples of how different methods of instruction can be used to develop applications that take advantage of multimedia hardware capabilities. Examples are also provided on how these applications were used as both a teaching tool and a learning tool. Figure 5-2 graphically represents these models of instruction and methods of use.

	Instructional Design Model				
Method of Use	Didactic Presentation	Exploration	Structured Observation	Simulated Interaction	Assessment & Instruction
Model T Teaching Tool	Understanding Groups	SE Asian Refugees American Indians	SE Asian Refugees Communication Skills	American Indians	
Model L Learning Tool	Understanding Groups	SE Asian Refugees American Indians	SE Asian Refugees Communication Skills	Problem Solving American Indians	Understanding Groups Descriptive Statistics

Figure 5.2 **An Integrated Model for Instructional Design and Use**

The first application produced for use in the college curriculum was *Understanding Groups in Education and the Human Services*. This application provided instruction on group dynamics and makes liberal use of video examples of group activities relevant to education and human services (Carlson & Falk, 1987). A second application on *Descriptive Statistics* covers basic statistical concepts, central tendency, and variance, with a mentor using computer text and graphics and video and still examples to expose students to concepts, to test their knowledge, and to provide remediation when necessary.

The third and fourth applications help learners in *Understanding Human Diversity*, with one disc focusing on Southeast Asian refugees and the other emphasizing American Indians (Falk & Carlson, 1990). These discs provide case examples of interacting with culturally different peoples, present background information on their culture, offer the opportunity to "visit" with people from different cultures, provide the learners opportunities to explore their own and others' values in a confidential manner, and present a theoretical framework for understanding diversity and its effects.

The development of the final four curriculum applications was funded by a grant from the McKnight Foundation. They are designed to provide in-service and pre-service education to enhance skills essential to human service professionals. One of the applications covers seven steps of *Problem Solving in the Human Services*, with learners participating in a case study involving a pregnant teenager and her family. Two of the four discs comprise an integrated application on *Communication Skills*, which focus on responding to content, feeling, and meaning; they include numerous video examples of people communicating in a variety of educational and human service settings. The final application on *Assessment in the Human Services* provides the opportunity for learners to develop the important skill of identifying human needs present in real-life situations involving individuals and families.

Video-enhanced didactic presentations In the *Understanding Groups* application, learners are (1) exposed to the name of a concept related to group dynamics, (2) presented with a definition, and (3) provided with one or more video examples of the group behavior that reflects that concept. Concepts and information about groups come alive with the incorporation of video and other multimedia capabilities.

The *Understanding Groups* application is being used as both a teaching tool and a learning tool. Instructors use portions of the application in a social work classroom to provide video examples of specific aspects of group leadership and group goals. Undergraduate honors students use the application to teach pre-service teachers about these same group dynamics. Elementary teacher education students use the application as a learning tool exploring group dynamics individually and in groups outside the classroom (Carlson & Falk, 1990).

Exploration. Categories of information are often linked to one another through the use of hypertext or icons that move the learner through the application, enabling a relatively free flowing discovery of the application's contents. Two disc sides on *Understanding Human Diversity* focusing on *Southeast Asian Refugees* and on *American Indians* expose learners to language, religion, historic background, lifestyles, and other aspects of a culture as they choose. Learners can explore American Indian treaties, information on the geography of Southeast Asia, traditional Indian medicines, simulated interaction with a Hmong woman and a Vietnamese man, the Ojibwe Indian language, and numerous other aspects of two other cultures.

The *Understanding Human Diversity* applications are also used as both teaching tools and learning tools in an exploration mode (Falk, 1988). Instructors use the application in class, introducing the application, its contents, and navigation to students, and then allowing students to direct the exploration of various aspects of the other cultures. Students also use the application on their own to explore the range of topics on two cultures quite distinct from their own.

Structured observation. In the *Communication Skills* application, learners are asked to use specific criteria to observe and rate video segments of discussions between two persons and then to compare and contrast their own observations and ratings to those of a mentor. In one application, a video segment of a teacher interacting with a family newly arrived from Southeast Asia, which focuses on understanding human diversity, learners observe and record culturally appropriate and inappropriate behaviors.

Each of the applications exemplifying structured observation can be used as either a teaching or a learning tool. In class, a teacher could use the *Communication Skills* application to have all students observe a video segment of two-way communication, and ask the students to record their observations. Then, the teacher could provide observations for comparison and contrast. The *Human Diversity* application could be used in the same way. Both applications could also be used outside of class, where students, either individually or in small groups, can be introduced to what they will observe, watch a video segment, receive information from the application on what occurred in the segment, and then compare and contrast their own observations with those shared in the application.

Simulated personal interaction. In the *Problem Solving in the Human Services* application, the learner takes the role of a social worker and interacts with a family experiencing problems. The choices that the learner makes influence both the family's behavior and the feedback received from the supervisor. In the second application aimed at *Understanding Human Diversity*, the learner selects from available questions and receives appropriate responses from an American Indian physician or from a traditional medicine man.

Each of these examples could also be used in class or as a learning tool outside of class. Because of the personal nature of interaction that is simulated, the learning tool use involves students more fully. It is very possible, however, for an entire class to participate in choosing which questions to ask the American Indian physician and the traditional medicine man and then to hear the responses as a group.

Assessment and focused instruction. The *Understanding Groups* application includes a pre-test, with a recommendation that learners go to either basic instruction or to a quicker review based on the pre-test performance. The *Descriptive Statistics* disc incorporates a test after an initial instructional activity, and students are directed to a remedial loop if they do not demonstrate a mastery of the tested concept.

This instructional model is more suited to use as a learning tool. It is as individuals that students receive a particular score on a test and are properly placed in the instruction. Individual performance also either demonstrates a mastery or not, determining whether remedial instruction is necessary. The fact that the

Understanding Groups application was also used as a learning tool for video-enhanced didactic instruction in the example above also indicates that a single application can include more than one model of instruction and can be used in different ways.

Guidelines

1. When generating ideas for how multimedia could be used as an effective instructional tool, consider several instructional models as possibilities. Video-enhanced didactic presentations, exploration, structured observation, simulated personal interaction, and assessment and focused instruction have all proven to be effective models.

2. Consider also that the multimedia can be used as either learning or teaching tools.

3. Multimedia can be used effectively as a learning tool either by individuals or in a small group.

4. Any combination of instructional models and methods of use may be particularly suited to a particular educational problem. Match the instructional model and method of use to the goals and objectives of the instruction and the characteristics of the learners.

5. Continue to seek new models of instruction and methods for using multimedia. The models and methods emphasized in this chapter are by no means exhaustive.

6. Whenever possible, view and use multimedia applications to get ideas for additional models of instruction.

7. Whenever possible, watch other people using multimedia as an instructional tool. You probably have years of experiencing lectures as a means of instruction; seek out opportunities to experience multimedia as a means of instruction.

Resources

The best way to become aware of the instructional models that can be used in multimedia applications is to see and use as many applications as you can. Many of the vendors and distributors mentioned in Chapter 6 will allow instructors to preview multimedia applications before purchase. Conferences focusing on multimedia and other learning technologies, such as SALT and AECT, have a variety of exhibits that feature multimedia applications and hardware; applications outside your discipline can provide ideas for models of instruction even if the content is not relevant to your interests. Increasingly, conferences in a variety of disciplines include sessions and exhibits on multimedia that are relevant as models for both instructional method and content.

Books and journals can also provide ideas for models to include in multimedia instruction. Books by Schwier and Misanchuk (1993), Daynes (1987), Arwady and Gayeski (1989), Perlmutter (1991), Iuppa (1990) and Iuppa and Anderson (1988) are among those that will provide alternatives to those presented in this chapter. Articles in journals such as *Educational Technology, Educational Technology Research and Development, Journal of Educational Multimedia and Hypermedia, Journal of Educational Technology Systems, Journal of Multimedia Computing, T.H.E. Journal, Multimedia Review,* and *Instructional Delivery Systems* may also provide ideas about models for instruction that take advantage of multimedia's capabilities.

Observing how instructors use multimedia can provide insights on how you might use this tool for instruction. College faculty and administrators often have no formal training in teaching, and we often teach as we were taught. Because few current faculty members experienced multimedia instruction as students, new models are required. You may observe or talk to colleagues in other disciplines on your own campus or seek out colleagues on other campuses for observation and discussion in using multimedia in instruction.

Chapter 10 provides information on how to use multimedia as a teaching tool in the classroom and as a learning tool for students outside of the classroom.

Conclusion

Multimedia hardware provides remarkable capabilities, but informed instructional design and use of applications and hardware are necessary to make multimedia an effective tool for teaching and learning. This chapter describes models for instruction and methods for using multimedia, providing new ways to think about multimedia instruction.

The next step is to actually obtain a multimedia application that can be used in instruction. There are three basic ways of acquiring an application: buying one that someone else developed, developing your own, or modifying applications developed by others. These three ways are covered in the next three chapters.

CHAPTER 6

GENERATING SOLUTIONS: PURCHASING OR OBTAINING EXISTING APPLICATIONS

Goals

The most direct way to obtain a multimedia solution to an identified educational problem is to purchase or otherwise gain access to an application developed by someone else. In order to find a solution in this way, you must know about the potential sources of multimedia applications and understand the methodology of determining whether an application is suitable for use in your particular situation. This chapter addresses both of these issues.

General Information

The number of multimedia applications in general, and those appropriate for use in higher education specifically, are growing rapidly. The *Videodisc Compendium for Education and Training*, an effective initial effort to catalog the variety of multimedia applications, lists over 2,000 videodisc titles and approximately 600 CD-ROM titles. *CD-ROM in Print* lists about 3,500 compact disc titles. Increasing numbers of CD-I applications are coming on the market, and DVI and other digitized video applications will be growing in both number and quality.

Sources of Multimedia Applications

Multimedia applications can be obtained in a number of ways. Increasingly, vendors and distributors are selling applications that come to them from a variety of sources. Some publishers now provide multimedia applications as a peripheral resource when textbooks are adopted for high enrollment courses. Some multimedia applications can also be obtained directly from universities or other developers who are not actively marketing their applications through an established vendor. Each of these sources is described generally in the paragraphs that follow; specific examples appear in the "Resources" section of this chapter.

Vendors and distributors. A number of vendors and distributors are now adding multimedia to the products that they carry. These vendors often have catalogs of multimedia applications, with the applications either listed separately or in the context of other audiovisual or computer software products. Vendors often specialize in the disciplines within which they produce and/or carry multimedia titles.

Textbook publishers. Textbook publishers have steadily increased the number and variety of peripheral learning aids for departments and instructors that adopt texts for high enrollment courses. Consequently, videodisc and CD-ROM applications have been added to other learning aids such as instructor manuals and computer test item banks as free resources that accompany larger textbook orders. These applications are most plentiful for subjects that typically have large introductory courses, such as psychology, biology, history, and political science. Portions of these applications may also be useful for more advanced courses.

Universities and other developers. Numerous colleges and universities have developed multimedia applications over the past decade (Kearsley, 1991), and some of these applications may be available only from those institutions. Consortia of universities have also been developed with each member institution contributing toward the development of an entire application or a particular portion. Your school may be able to join a consortium and obtain its applications, or purchase applications from existing consortia.

Process to Follow in Obtaining Multimedia Applications

The general problem solving process and instructional design activities provide guidance for considering possible multimedia applications. This process is described below.

Step 1: Review the educational problem. Examine the original instructional goal and the nature of the educational setting, the learner characteristics, and the learning objectives related to that goal. Keep these aspects of the educational problem in mind when identifying sources and previewing multimedia applications.

Step 2: Identify sources of multimedia applications. Use the general sources described above and the specific sources identified in the resource section of this chapter as starting points. Look for those sources that emphasize the topics you desire for college students and other adult learners. At this point there are far more videodisc and CD-ROM applications available than any other types of distributed multimedia applications.

Step 3: Preview possible multimedia applications. Obtain specific applications that appear to address directly the identified educational problem. Previewing obviously requires that you have available the hardware needed to run the application. If the hardware is not available on one's own campus, other local colleges might allow another faculty member to use their equipment, or some vendors might provide the equipment on request. In addition to considering the type of hardware actually necessary to deliver the multimedia instruction, the instructional models incorporated in the application should be noted.

Step 4: Anticipate how the application will be used. The application might be used as either a learning tool outside of the classroom or as a in-class teaching tool. It might function as a remedial tool for those having difficulties in a class, for enrichment, or as a central portion of the instruction on a given topic (see Chapter 4). The goal at this point is to generate as many ways as possible of using the application.

Step 5: Examine the advantages and disadvantages of the potential application. Chapter 9 provides a number of criteria to consider when weighing the advantages and disadvantages of a particular multimedia application in relation to other multimedia applications and to other learning activities. The focus in this chapter is to be aware of all the possible multimedia options. Chapter 9 provides greater emphasis on deciding whether to actually obtain and then use the application.

Step 6: Decide whether to use the multimedia application. After weighing the advantages and disadvantages of using an existing multimedia application, one must then decide whether to obtain and use that product (see Chapter 9). If a particular multimedia application appears to address a particular educational problem better than the available alternatives, both multimedia and other, the question answers itself. Then, you must ascertain whether the required hardware is in place (Chapter 4), decide how to use the application (Chapter 5), provide the multimedia instruction (Chapter 10), and evaluate whether the instruction effectively addressed the identified educational problem (Chapter 11).

If you decide that no existing application seems appropriate, but believe that a multimedia solution would be effective in addressing the specific educational problem, you could either develop an application of your own (Chapter 7) or repurpose an existing application (Chapter 8). If multimedia now seems inappropriate for the educational problem at hand, instruction can be provided in another manner.

Questions

The questions listed below provide guidance for generating options for purchasing or otherwise obtaining multimedia applications:

1. What is the educational problem to be addressed by the multimedia application?

   What is the instructional goal?

   What are the characteristics of the learners?

   What are the learning objectives?

2. What are possible sources of relevant multimedia applications?

   — Vendors?

   — Textbook publishers?

   — Other universities or colleges?

3. What hardware is necessary to use the application? Is it currently available? Could it be obtained?
4. What are the instructional models within the application? Are they appropriate to the educational problem and instructional goals?
5. What are the advantages and disadvantages of the application compared to other applications and other instructional options?
6. How could the application be used?
    — As a teaching tool?
    — As a learning tool?
    — As a core part of instruction?
    — As remediation?
    — As enrichment?
7. How much does the application cost?

Examples

The example offered below follows the complete process just described. A number of examples of multimedia applications selected for particular disciplines are described, but the complete process reflected in the first example is not repeated.

The Process of Reviewing an Application

Step 1: Review the educational problem. The general instructional goals of a course on human diversity are for pre-service teacher education students to (1) understand differences among people in the United States, (2) understand different forms of discrimination, and (3) know ways in which people have worked over the years to eliminate discrimination. The instructional task is to expose students to information on these topics in such a way as to provide information related to these goals while at the same time to move students emotionally through the topics. Most of the students are nineteen and twenty years old and from white, middle-class backgrounds. Having been born in the 1970s, these students have limited knowledge of the Civil Rights Movement and its leaders. The learning objectives for a specific portion of the instruction are for students to be able to (1) identify key civil rights leaders, (2) describe the philosophies of key leaders, and (3) list key events in the Civil Rights Movement.

Step 2: Identify sources of multimedia applications. A review of the *1994 Videodisc Compendium* indicates a number of videodisc applications that address this topic; many of these applications, however, are aimed at elementary or secondary students. IBM markets Martin Luther King's "Letter from a Birmingham Jail" as part of its Ultimedia *Illuminated Manuscripts* application. Two videodisc applications on human diversity are available that were developed on campus: one focuses on American Indians and the other on Southeast Asian refugees. A review of *CD-ROMs in Print* and literature from various publishers indicates that no other possible applications exist that offer better potential to address the educational problem.

Step 3: Preview possible multimedia applications. ABC Interactive developed the videodisc application *Martin Luther King, Jr.* and markets it through Optical Media, and one can preview this application free of charge using a Macintosh computer and one of several videodisc players. The application can also be used with a bar code reader. The *Illuminated Manuscripts'* "Letter from a Birmingham Jail" comes packaged with four other manuscripts for a total cost of over $2,500 and requires sophisticated hardware, so this option was not pursued.

Step 4: Anticipate how the application could be used. The *Martin Luther King, Jr.* application could be used in a variety of ways. Some segments could function as a teaching tool in the classroom with the instructor selecting and presenting those portions relevant to the instructional goals and objectives. The application could also be used as one of several enrichment options that students could pursue in a laboratory outside of class, either being guided through particular portions of the application or exploring it on their own.

Step 5: Examine the advantages and disadvantages of the potential application. The *Martin Luther King, Jr.* application has several advantages, including a variety of resources (text, video, stills, and documents) for each of the topics related to the educational goals, the ability to cover topics in greater or lesser depth, ease of use, and relatively low cost ($395). Disadvantages include material geared primarily to a younger age group (secondary students) and limited coverage of other civil rights leaders.

Step 6: Decide whether to use the multimedia application. Advantages of the *Martin Luther King, Jr* application outweigh its disadvantages. This application has been used, in fact, both as a teaching tool for teacher education students and as a learning tool where students explore relevant topics independently outside of class. The initial evaluations indicate that the students achieve the content objectives and find the instruction valuable; as a side benefit at the same time, they enjoy experiencing multimedia as an instructional tool.

The example above provides an overview of a complete process for reviewing existing multimedia applications and deciding whether to obtain a particular application. The sections below list and, in some cases, describe very briefly individual applications available within various disciplines. The listed costs, with educational discounts sometimes available, generally come from the *1994 Videodisc Compendium* or other information provided by distributors, and are subject to change.

Examples of Applications in the Sciences

Biology. A number of applications centered around videodiscs are available in biology. The *BioSci II* application ($695), an updated version of a pioneer application developed by Videodiscovery, includes over 7,000 still photos, 100 movie sequences, 500 computer graphics, and 30 animations on life science topics such as biochemistry, botany, reproduction, ecology, and genetics. Dissections of frogs, fetal pigs, earthworms, mussels, squid, crayfish, sea stars, and perch are presented in labeled, unlabeled, and quiz formats, offering an effective, practical, and morally acceptable alternative to in-class dissection. *Cell Biology*, also by Videodiscovery ($695), provides 85 video sequences and over 200 high-resolution still images of the inner processes of the living cell.

Numerous other applications are available. *The Biology Encyclopedia* from Carolina Biological Supply ($550), *The Living Textbook-Life Science* from Optical Data Corporation ($1,495), *A World Alive* from Voyager ($50), and *Atoms to Anatomy: A Multimedia View of Human Systems* from Videodiscovery ($695) are all examples of Level III videodisc applications. *The Complete Audubon* from Creative Multimedia Corporation and *Mammals: A Multimedia Encyclopedia* from the National Geographic Society represent CD-ROM applications. *Life Story* uses QuickTime video segments and a videodisc to demonstrate the story behind the discovery of DNA.

Chemistry. A number of applications focus on chemistry. *Doing Chemistry* from the American Chemical Society ($595) includes 122 experiments and demonstrations. This videodisc application uses still frames to indicate the objectives, materials, experimental set-ups, and safety procedures as well as motion segments to demonstrate techniques best illustrated by example. *The Living Textbook-Cosmic Chemistry* from Optical Data Corporation ($1,595) also uses a variety of multimedia capabilities to provide comprehensive coverage of basic chemistry topics. Falcon Software provides videodisc and M-Motion applications on *Acids and Bases*, *Chemical Reactions and Solubilities*, and *Rates and Equilibrium* ($350 each for videodisc application, $500 each for M-Motion). Falcon Software also distributes the *Introductory Chemistry CD Package* on CD-ROM ($1,245).

Mathematics. A number of Level III applications provide individualized instruction appropriate for beginning level college math. These include the *Interactive Math Series* from Edutech Support Services ($4,185 for each of two disc applications), *Interactive Math: Probability and Statistics* from Miami-Dade Community College ($950), *Interactive Mathematics I and II* from Ferranti International ($5,400 each), and *Interactive ModuMath* and *Interactive ModuMath: Algebra* from the Wisconsin Foundation for Vocational, Technical, and Adult Education ($5,900 and $1,900 respectively).

Health sciences. A number of multimedia applications have been specifically designed for health sciences in higher education. *Slice of Life* videodiscs from Slice of Life ($150-$300) are visual encyclopedias or databases of over 60,000 still images pertaining to medicine, nursing, dentistry, and allied health on topics that include cardiology, gross anatomy, histology, microbiology, neuroanatomy, pathology, and other clinical disciplines. Software for these videodisc applications costs from $100 to $200. Some applications focus on clinical disciplines, such as *Anatomy and Physiology of the Heart* by the British Columbia Institute of Technology ($895), *Basic Hematology* by Datastar Educational Systems ($1,295), *Histology, A Photographic Atlas* from Image Premastering ($535), and

Gross Anatomy of the Neck by the Health Sciences Consortium ($1,300). Other applications focus on particular health/medical problems, including *Cyanotic Premature Babies* from the Health Science Consortium ($1,300), *Abdominal Stab Wounds* from Darox Interactive ($1,695), and *Urinary Bladder Pathology* from Intellipath ($550).

Other Sciences. Multimedia applications are also available for other sciences. Astronomy applications on videodisc include *The Living Textbook-Astronomy and the Sun* ($1,495) and *Voyager Gallery:Space Disc Vol. 1* ($195) from Optical Data Corporation; and on CD-ROM include *Amazing Universe* from Hopkins Technology ($80) and *The View from the Earth* from Warner New Media ($80). Geology applications include *The Living Textbook-Geology and Meteorology* from Optical Data Corporation ($995) and *Planet Earth: The Earth Within* from Coronet/MTI ($235-$325). *Physics Vignettes* from John Wiley & Sons ($175) and *The Living Textbook-Physical Science* ($1,495) are examples of physics applications.

Examples of Applications in the Social Sciences.

History. Numerous Level III videodisc applications focus on history. *The American History Videodisc* from Instructional Resources Corporation ($595) includes almost 3,000 images of American history, 10 narrated overviews, and 68 full-motion video segments. *Images of the French Revolution* from G. K. Hall ($450) includes 38,000 images on various topics related to this momentous period. *IBM Columbus: Encounter, Discovery and Beyond* ($2,857) includes stills, motion, graphics, and text on three videodiscs and two CD-ROM as it explores the life, events, and times of Columbus and the impact of his voyages and discoveries. Other videodisc titles include *Lessons of War* from ABC Interactive, *History in Motion: Milestones of the 20th Century* ($595) and the *Video Encyclopedia of the 20th Century* ($10,990) from CEL Educational Resources, and *The Western Civilization Videodisc* and *The World History (Non-European History)* from the Instructional Resources Corporation ($595 each).

Numerous CD-ROM titles also are available. *History of the World* from Bureau Development ($795) is a research and reference tool presenting HarperCollins textbooks, and *North American Indians* from Quanta ($129) is a text/image database on the history of Native Americans covering leadership, tribal heritage, religion, family life, and customs. Bureau Development also offers *Biographies* ($200), offering approximately one hundred biographies of famous people with voice-overs and hundreds of color images, and *U. S. History* ($395), which provides a social, economic, political, military, and scientific history of the United States from the 1600s to current by presenting the full text of 107 books and hundreds of pictures, illustrations, and tables. Other CD-ROM titles include *Atlas of the U.S. Presidents* from Applied Optical Media ($40), *Desert Storm: The War in the Persian Gulf* from Warner New Media ($40), and a series of titles on *USA Wars* from Quanta Press ($70-$129).

Other social sciences. Political science titles include *The '88 Vote* by ABC Interactive ($395) and *The 1992 Time Magazine Compact Almanac-Multimedia Edition* from Compact Publishing ($195), a CD-ROM application that includes 15,000 articles on major political and other events of the twentieth century. Geography CD-ROM titles include *Countries of the World* from Bureau Development ($395) and *American Vista* and *World Vista* from Applied Optical Media ($80 each). Generic psychology videodiscs and software can be obtained as resources from publishers such as West Publishing and HarperCollins with the adoption of their text for introductory courses.

Examples of Applications in the Fine Arts

Art. Videodisc applications on art typically focus on either a particular artist or a specific museum. Examples of the former include *Van Gogh Revisited* ($130) and *Michelangelo: Self-Portrait* ($160) from Voyager. Voyager also distributes a three-videodisc collection of almost 30,000 still frames and over seventy narrated sequences of the paintings and drawings, sculptures and objets d'art, and antiquities from *The Louvre* ($295) and another application from the *National Gallery of Art*, which includes a single videodisc produced by Videodisc Publishing ($160). An example of a CD-ROM application is the *Coates Art Review: Impressionism* from Quanta Press ($129).

Music. Voyager and Warner New Media have both developed a series of CD-based multimedia applications that incorporate text and graphics to provide context, criticism, commentary, and perspective on classical works of music. *Mozart's Dissonant Quartet* by Voyager ($150) combines performance, musical demonstrations, still-frame images, and commentary on videodisc with a multi-tiered computer program/CD-ROM to present a fully interactive exploration of Mozart's masterpiece of chamber music. The application allows the student to explore Mozart's life and world, watch the Angeles Quartet perform, and see and hear various musical instruments. Other titles in the CD Companion Series from Voyager include *Beethoven: Symphony No. 9*, *Stravinsky: The Rite of Spring*, *Schubert: "The Trout" Quintet*, and *Strauss: Three Tone Poems* (about $70-$100 each).

Warner New Media offers similar CD applications. Mozart's *The Magic Flute* offers text and graphics on the composer's life and times and allows the user to view the German lyrics, an English translation, and notes on the music and plot while listening to the opera. Other Warner titles include *A German Requiem*, *The Orchestra*, and *The String Quartet No. 14* ($66-$80 each).

Examples of Applications in Various Other Disciplines

Business. Many multimedia applications originally developed for use in the workplace are also most appropriate for use in higher education. The *1994 Videodisc Compendium* lists over sixty Level III videodisc applications in this area, along with several CD-ROM applications. Vendors and distributors include Wilson Learning, Electrocom (in French), Interactive Instructional Systems, and the National Education and Training Group. Many of these applications are quite expensive (ranging up to $25,000 for a series of titles), but some are feasible for a higher education budget.

Foreign languages. A mix of videodisc and CD-ROM applications are available for common foreign languages. Videodisc applications include *The Connection Series* by Tannberg Educational, Inc. ($3,769) for French, German, and Spanish; *A Good Beginning* from Tell Systems International ($550) for English as a second language instruction; and *SETS Language Learning Disc* from SETS ($2,950), which covers generic language learning skills for any foreign language. CD-ROM titles include the *Berlitz Think and Talk* series from Hyperglot Software ($199 each) for French, German, Italian, and Spanish; *Eight Days in Paris* from Tannberg ($818 with educational discounts available); and the *Introductory Games in . . .* series from Syracuse Language Systems ($90 each) for French, German, Japanese, and Spanish.

Teacher education. A number of applications are directed at improving knowledge and skills related to teaching. The University of Alberta has developed three Level II videodisc applications in *Classroom Discipline: A Simulation Approach* ($175 Canadian), *Classroom Management: A Case Study Approach* ($150 Canadian), and *Do I Ask Effective Questions?* ($225 Canadian). Emerging Technology Consultants has produced seven applications to help teachers use new teaching and learning technologies effectively ($220-$755 each). Other videodisc titles include *Essential Teaching Skills* from Ferranti International ($2,800) and *Teaching With Groups!* from the Agency for Instructional Technology ($295).

Guidelines

1. When seeking possible multimedia applications, always keep in mind the nature of the educational problem to be addressed.
2. Seek possible applications from a variety of sources, including vendors, publishers, and other universities.
3. Take particular note of the instructional models that the application uses.
4. Brainstorm as many possible uses of the application as possible, considering its appropriateness as both a teaching tool and a learning tool.
5. Consider the advantages and disadvantages of the application in relation to other multimedia applications and other instructional options, using criteria presented in Chapter 9.
6. Use whatever means possible, including attending relevant conferences, previewing applications, and watching colleagues teach with multimedia, to obtain first-hand information about applications and their possible use.

Resources

This book's appendix lists numerous sources of multimedia applications. It highlights some of those sources, providing information about the types of applications emphasized. The vendor and distributor section of the appendix lists all the vendors and distributors noted earlier in this chapter, along with telephone numbers.

The best single source of existing multimedia applications incorporating videodiscs is the *Videodisc Compendium for Education and Training* from Emerging Technology, Inc. The 1994 edition lists over 2,800 titles in fourteen areas relevant to higher education. Included in the 1994 compendium are over 400 CD titles. Each listing provides a variety of information about the application, including a summary of the content, the publisher, cost, and age level to which the application is geared. Because of the rapid growth in this market, the publisher offers quarterly updates.

The most comprehensive single source for listing multimedia applications incorporating CD-ROM is *CD-ROMs in Print* published annually by the Mecklermedia Corporation. The 1993 version includes about 3,500 titles. This resource comes both in print format and as a CD-ROM. Another source of CD-ROM titles, geared to professional users, is *CD-ROM Finder*, published by Learned Information, Inc. In early 1995, Learned will publish *Key Guide to Electronic Information: Education*, a comprehensive directory of electronic sources of educational materials.

A number of distributors publish catalogs of existing applications, which can be obtained upon request. Videodiscovery specializes in applications covering life sciences, but distributes a variety of other titles. AIMS Media and Coronet/MTI focus on history, but have applications on a variety of other topics. Ztek and Educational Resources distribute applications in many areas. Voyager specializes in classic movies on videodisc and multimedia applications on art and music.

Several periodicals include reviews of applications on a regular basis. Examples of these journals include *Multimedia World, The World of Macintosh Multimedia, New Media, Multimedia Today, CD-ROM Professional*, and *CD-ROM World*.

Conferences within disciplines increasingly include papers, presentations, and exhibits focusing on multimedia as a technology that can affect the discipline. Check conference schedules and exhibits for information about multimedia applications.

Textbook publishers are increasingly offering multimedia applications as learning peripherals with certain texts used for large courses. Check with publishers' representatives for information on applications available.

Conclusion

With more and more multimedia applications becoming available almost daily, the opportunity for using off-the-shelf products continues to expand. Applications involving videodiscs are more prevalent, but CD-ROMs are increasingly being used for digital-based applications. In seeking appropriate titles, one must know the sources of existing applications and then systematically review the promising products to determine which will effectively address the educational problem identified. Finding a useful existing application is by far the quickest and least expensive approach to using multimedia as an instructional tool.

CHAPTER 7

GENERATING SOLUTIONS: DEVELOPING YOUR OWN MULTIMEDIA APPLICATIONS

Goals

As you determine the goals, instructional models, and instructional outcomes, it is important that you explore available multimedia options. If purchasing an application related to a particular topic or method is not possible, original multimedia programs can be developed. Because multimedia development is complex and costly, this option is usually a last resort solution.

In developing an original multimedia application, one must first remember the general problem solving steps: (1) define the problem, (2) generate alternative solutions, (3) examine alternative solutions and select a solution, (4) implement the solution selected, and (5) evaluate whether the solution solved the problem. One option for generating alternative solutions is developing your own application from "scratch." This step (after defining the problem) involves (1) specialized design of instruction, (2) production and mastering of the multimedia program, (3) completion of the computer program, (4) development of appropriate documentation, and (5) specialized formative evaluation. These steps are usually completed by a team of professionals, each with distinctive and essential roles—manager, instructional designers, production personnel, computer programmers, and evaluators.

This chapter describes the various steps and roles, providing an overview of the process of developing applications. These range from comprehensive, professionally produced videodisc or CD-ROM programs to instructor-developed classroom programs digitized on a hard disc. The more in-depth knowledge provided in this chapter's "Resources" section should be consulted for additional information before beginning any application development project.

General Background

The Process of Development — A Look at the Literature

General principles of multimedia development have been suggested. For example, DeBloois (1982) discusses defining a purpose based on an analysis of learner's needs. Choice of viewing motion or still images, interacting and obtaining feedback, or participating in simulations that require decision making should be offered to learners. Floyd & Floyd (1982) discuss a process orientation in which the selection and sequence of messages is determined by the user's response to the material. Iuppa (1990) considers instructional design, flowcharting, and program design.

Bayard-White (1988) has developed questions to guide the process of original multimedia development. These include commissioning organization, first steps (why multimedia, budget/resources), pre-production (needs analysis/aims/objectives, learning/training strategies, delivery system), production (audiovisual material), and programming. To illustrate the answers the questions raise, case studies of original disc development in such areas as foreign language learning are given using a common outline—background, first steps, pre-production, production, post-production/editing, project management, implementation, and evaluation.

Bergman and Moore (1990) suggest that the developer must define multimedia applications, build the project team, plan the project, design the application, develop and document the design, produce the media, author the program, and validate the application. Managing the project includes consideration of a project control book with personnel assignments, project schedules and budget (planning, intermediate, and final), approvals and sign-offs, and other records. Project managers need to have checklists for evaluating each phase of the process as well as agreed-upon storyboard forms.

Tasks in the Development of Multimedia Programs

As in the development of all instruction using multimedia, the necessary first step involves carefully defining the problem. This includes analyzing the characteristics of the setting and the learners as well as developing general goals for instruction. It is also helpful to consider other alternatives, as discussed in Chapters 6 and 8, before proceeding.

Combining ideas from the literature cited above, five major task areas are involved in developing original instructional software for interactive technologies: (1) specialized design of the instructional program, (2) production and mastering of the multimedia or videotape, (3) completion of the computer program, (4) development of documentation, and (5) specialized evaluation of the instructional package. These tasks are often divided among the group members fulfilling the roles described below: manager, instructional designers, production experts, and computer programmers. Or they can be accomplished by one person who has the required knowledge and experience in each of the roles.

Specialized design of instructional programs. After the overall project goals and plans are developed and a project team assembled, the needed resources are delineated and monies obtained, often through the writing of grant proposals. Because no industry-wide standards exist, it is necessary to select the hardware and software that will handle the chosen application. Subject matter experts are interviewed, the potential audience for the instruction is surveyed, and relevant literature is reviewed.

Designing the instructional program requires that specific objectives and content chunks be clearly described and a general plan for instruction be developed. This general plan is graphically represented in what is termed a gross flowchart. Next, instructional techniques with the appropriate mix of media (graphics, still and rolling video, text, and/or overlays) are determined. Finally precise scripts and computer branching is decided and recorded on Level Two flowcharts and storyboards. Each step offers opportunities for subject matter experts to review the material and to suggest revisions.

Production and mastering of the multimedia application. The pre-production process begins as the instructional designers consider the mix of media that would most successfully complement the material to be learned. Production experts suggest various alternatives and techniques, particularly those that result in more involvement on the part of the learner. For analog applications using videodiscs, production taping can be accomplished at either a studio or remote location. A director is responsible for actors' interactions, sets and props, and the technicians tasks. Video rolling sequences and stills as well as scripts for the second audio track (for videodiscs) are taped. After production, editing of appropriate material onto a master tape occurs. Careful review of a rough cut edit precedes the final edit. This step is followed by "mastering," where the material is transferred to a multimedia system or sound cue coding is added to the videotape.

For digitized applications, information is compiled onto the computer's hard disk by capturing original production or clips from already produced tapes or by scanning material from "stills" into the program. The contents of the hard disk can then be mastered onto a CD-ROM disc.

Completion of the computer program. If a Level Three videodisc application is desired, programming begins when the storyboards are being completed. Computer programmers bring software issues to the attention of the designers and provide insight into the effects of various programming choices on particular sequences of instruction. The programmers may use a programming language such as Pascal, that is usable on a variety of hardware configurations. Authoring systems or languages also are available, which may simplify but also restrict the programming process. Programs allow a series of frames created by the author, whether they be text, graphics, questions, instructions, or video sequences, to be combined into a coherent whole. The types of user services (help screens, glossary, control over video) also are programmed. After review, computer programmers complete editing changes. See Chapter 8 (pp 93-95) for more information about programming.

Completion of appropriate documentation. As the instructional design is being completed, the work on appropriate documentation begins. This often involves the development of a learner manual and an instructor manual. The learner manual describes the hardware and gives directions about its use. The manual may be coordinated with the multimedia program, where the learner will be asked to record various observations or comments about the interactions contained in the video sequences. The instructor manual can give additional examples of activities and discussions related to the instructional program. It can also contain learner evaluation tools.

Specialized formative evaluation and beta testing. Formative evaluation, which seeks to answer questions related to the improvement of the instructional program, occurs as learners use the multimedia application. If learners are carefully observed as they complete the instruction and notes are taken, changes can be made to improve effectiveness. Learners may also complete written evaluations of the disk program. See Chapter 11 for more detailed information about evaluation.

Roles of the Project Team Members

To develop instructional programs for the new technologies requires a design team with each member's role clearly defined, but with a common goal—the creation of an excellent instructional program. Both individual accountability and overall cooperation and collaboration are needed to achieve a useful final instructional product. Four roles are important in the design team—manager, instructional designer(s), production personnel, and computer programmer(s). In addition, the project needs an evaluator, both within and without the design team. Each of these roles is examined in more detail below.

Manager. The design team manager carries specific responsibilities. Within the design team, the manager organizes tasks and facilitates positive interpersonal interactions, maintaining a balance of task and maintenance behaviors, using effective communication skills and applying peaceful conflict resolution techniques. The manager also provides liaison with the external community. For example, the manager may have to relate to other administrators in the university or in another organization in which the design team is housed. Further, the manager may serve as the contact person with the instructional program's intended audience or funding agency.

Instructional designers. After the team defines the problem, the instructional designers move forward with the creation of specific objectives and content chunks of the instructional program. They also decide on the most effective way to present particular content to the learner. They need to be experts in creating gross and Level Two flowcharts as well as storyboards. Other responsibilities include the development of manuals to accompany the multimedia or videotape and the evaluation of the instruction.

Production experts. Production experts share in determining how best to portray each aspect of the video production. Whether shots are to be wide-angle or cutaways, whether a portable steady cam or a still camera should be used, whether a special effects rolling video should be incorporated within another rolling sequence—these are the decisions of the production expert in consultation with the instructional designers. For interactive technologies, the production expert also needs to film sequences so that they seem naturally rolling as a single sequence and, at the same time, offer the possibility of using each single segment in other ways. How engaging and engrossing a program becomes often depends on the skills of the production expert.

Computer programmers. Computer programmers take the Level Two flowcharts and the storyboards of the instructional designers and convert them into Level Three charts that reflect the branching directions the programmer needs. The programmer may use a variety of authoring programs, systems, or languages to implement the branching tracks to the audio, video, or other combinations suggested by the instructional designers. Graphics and text, both alone and as overlays, are added by the computer programmer.

Collaboration between design team members and other constituencies. Interactive multimedia, such as multimedia with Level Three interactivity, can be expensive to produce. Project managers often need to interact with funding agencies or companies in response to calls for proposals or to report on design progress. Managers of design teams are often middle-level managers, such as department heads or deans, who need to communicate with higher level administrators in their institutions, such as vice-chancellors, chancellors, and presidents. Whatever the meeting, these managers are most effective when they practice basic principles of collaboration and cooperation.

Instructional designers meet with subject matter experts in a variety of ways. They may interview individual subject matter experts with a standard set of questions. They may meet with small or large group advisory boards for their ideas on content important to a particular program. Designers may also use a written survey with large numbers of subject matter experts and engage in a nominal group process to set priorities for content and objectives for a disc. In each of these instances, a collaborative/cooperative model is essential (Carlson & Nierengarten, 1989).

Production experts meet with instructional designers at two key points: first, at the early stages of the design when initial questions are raised and suggestions shared related to the appropriate media treatments of various content areas; second, a month prior to production, when final details are discussed and storyboard directions to producers and actors are refined.

The production experts meet with the actors, sometimes with the instructional designers present, to review the script, to describe differences between linear and interactive production, and to rehearse the dialogues. Again, use of the collaborative/cooperative model creates both a positive interpersonal climate and goal achievement.

Computer programmers are aware of the new authoring systems, languages, and other programming languages and often need to meet with technical experts to discuss and debate the merits of various hardware choices. In an era in which no common standards for interactive technologies seem to exist, continual evaluation of programming directions is imperative. Again, a collaborative model is useful, particularly in the area of problem solving, where various options and their consequences can be considered.

In smaller projects, which focus on students developing instructional materials for other learners, the roles and steps in production may be combined in various ways with fewer people needing to be involved.

Questions

To complete an original multimedia program, specific questions need to be addressed. The main questions are listed below.

1. Has the educational problem been clearly defined? (See Chapter 3 for more information about defining the problem.)
   Has the project developed overall goals and plans?
   Has the project team been assembled?
   Have adequate resources been secured?
   Has hardware been selected?
   Have subject matter experts been interviewed?
   Has the potential audience of students been surveyed?
   Has the relevant literature been reviewed?

2. Has the design of instruction been completed?
   Related to goals and objectives, have the content chunks been written?
   Has the overall multimedia program organization been determined?
   Has the gross flowchart been developed?
   Have the appropriate media and resources been selected?
   Has the Level Two flowchart been developed?
   Have the storyboards been written that describe graphics, audio, video, text, and branching?
   Have appropriate times for review and revision been carried out?

3. Has the production and mastering process been completed?
   Have the appropriate mix of media been selected?
   Have the actors (if needed) been located and trained?
   Have the props/art cards/stills been developed?
   Have the video (if needed) sequences been taped?
   Have the audio sequences been taped?
   Has a rough cut edit been accomplished?
   Has the final edit been completed?
   Has the mastering to disk or conversion to DVI been done?

4. Has the computer programming been completed?
   Has the appropriate authoring language or programming language been selected?
   Have programming issues been discussed with other team members?
   Have audio, video, stills, graphics, or text been combined into the computer program?

Have all the sequences and branches been completed as outlined on the storyboards?

Has editing been completed based on feedback?

5. Has the documentation been developed?

Has a learner manual been created and tested?

Has the instructor manual been created and tested?

Have directions for use been clearly written?

6. Has the evaluation of the instructional program been completed? (See Chapter 11 for more information about the evaluation.)

7. If a team is used, has a cooperative team process been used?

Example One

A group of faculty members preparing students for human service professionals wanted to help them gain skills in communication. After examining all the issues, the group decided that the best response to the educational problem was to create an original multimedia instructional program.

Specialized Design of Instruction

In defining the educational problem—using multimedia in teaching future human service professionals basic concepts about effective communication—the design team worked with a group of subject matter experts and, using a nominal group process, identified several goals, objectives, and content chunks. These goals included effective ways to respond to the content, feelings, and meaning of another person. Projected content chunks included demonstrations of paraphrasing as well as responding to the category and intensity of feelings of another person. There were varieties of situations for reaction and rating, mentor comments, and scenario-based pre- and post-tests.

Because no multimedia applications were available to fulfill these goals and objectives, the design team decided to produce an original instructional program. The instructional designers created gross flowcharts, Level Two flowcharts, and storyboards for each aspect of the content. For example, to facilitate learning about effective and ineffective communication, the designers created scenarios of interaction typical of human service professionals—teacher-pupil interactions in classrooms, social worker interactions with clients, parent-teacher conferences, and colleague interactions. Inclusion of multi-cultural perspectives in describing effective communication was considered important. Scripts for actors were created. Designs for the graphics and still images were developed.

The following are examples of each of the main design components for responding to feelings:

1. The gross flowchart shows the overall organization of the disc. There are two main sections—learning basic concepts and evaluating response effectiveness plus a conclusion.

2. The Level Two flowchart shows greater detail of a single component part. Each space in the flowchart would show a particular topic and its relationship to the design as a whole.

3. The storyboards illustrate the relationship of audio, video, and computer graphics as well as the branching if a Level Three program is to be developed.

Production and Mastering of the Multimedia Application

The design team production experts located actors from the university's theater department and coached them for the script. The production experts also worked with the director of the media resources center. This center owned sets appropriate for the scripted scenes and was staffed with production teams to complete the sets, operate the cameras, and create the lighting and other effects. Filming was also done on location.

Copies of the scenarios filmed on the one-inch production tape were made. These were reviewed by the group of subject matter experts. For example, one scenario included a focus on cross-cultural communication. A Latino teenager, following the norms for his culture, appeared to be disrespectful to his middle-class white teacher. The interaction was carefully critiqued by representatives of both Latino and white cultures to make sure that the sequence was authentic and appropriate for analysis by learners. This process of careful critiquing was completed for each scenario. Refilming was done wherever necessary.

In addition to the moving scenarios, the production experts also located and arranged all the stills—slides, graphs, rating scales, etc. The items were filmed in the order that they would be mastered onto the disk.

The rough tapes were then edited, and needed transitions and fade-outs added. Because multimedia applications included many small segments and hundreds of stills, an "editing" organizational pattern was necessary. The editors followed this script carefully. After the editing was completed, the finished tape was sent out for mastering; in this case, the 3M facility handled that phase. The cost for the first master copy was $1800, with additional discs priced at $20 each. Another alternative would be to capture all of the material onto the computer's hard disk and send that for mastering onto a CD-ROM disc. Combinations of analog mastering on videodisc and digitized mastering on CD-ROM could also be done.

Completion of Appropriate Documentation

During production, the instructional designers created the documentation needed for the multimedia program. Here, an accompanying manual provided information about how to use the hardware, gave background to the instructor, and included role plays and simulations that could be used as follow-up material to that presented on the disk. Applying the critiquing skills learned through use of the multimedia application would be essential if the students were to internalize the new communication strategies.

*Completion of Computer Program and Specialized Formative
Evaluation*

Upon return of the disc, the computer programmers began their arduous task
using the storyboards created by the instructional designers. After programming
was competed (in the Pascal programming language) the software instructions
were compiled. As segments were completed, faculty and students would come
in to review the material and necessary changes would be made. These programming processes are more fully described in Chapter 8.

Example Two

Two students in a liberal education history class were working together to produce a visual essay about the history of their local area. After completing the
background reading, they talked together and completed a basic outline—they
would focus on the assimilation period (1880s through the 1920s) from the perspectives of various ethnic groups. The themes would include nature and technology, individualism and communal orientations, and assimilation and cultural
identity. They created a gross flowchart to show the relationship of chronology
and themes.

The students selected a variety of primary and secondary sources to complement the word-processed essay—maps, photographs, video excerpts, and original production. To make sure that everything fit well together, they completed a
series of storyboards that showed how the text, audio, and various visuals would
be organized.

Finally they were ready to use the Quadra 840 equipped with QuickTime
and SuperCard in the university's laboratory. Scanners, laser color printers, and
CD players were also connected to the system. The laboratory assistants
showed them how to access the user-friendly programs and to begin to complete this phase of the report. They scanned photographs into the report, selected appropriate and relevant maps from the Image Maker CD disc, and used the
video input to include clips from an oral history videotape. They conducted
original oral history video interviews with some of the community's older res-
idents from different cultures. They called in a few fellow students to review
the essay as it emerged and to offer ideas for improvement. Corrections were
made as suggested.

On the day scheduled for their presentation to the class, the students hooked
their product up to the LCD overhead. The combination of audio, visual, and
graphic components provided a coherent presentation. Class members, in evaluating the report, said that they learned more when the visuals (both still and moving) were a part of the report. The essay would be stored on disk for future classes, beginning a new kind of library.

Example Three

A professor was preparing a lecture for a course, International Perspectives in Early Childhood Education. After reviewing catalogs for available multimedia materials, she decided that some of her own materials could be developed into an original multimedia presentation.

Using Aldus Persuasion with connections to QuickTime, she developed an original program: color screens reflecting key points of her presentation, stills of early childhood programs in various countries, short digitized video clips of teacher-student interactions in early childhood settings in these countries, and charts (pie-graphs) summarizing research about how professionals in different countries view early childhood education.

The outline format templates of Aldus Persuasion served as a form of gross flow chart, while the data worksheets served as storyboards to organize the text, graphics, video, and sound. In developing this program, the professor combined the roles of instructional designer, manager, and producer. The software itself provided a framework for programming.

A portable hard disc stored the created program, which was then taken to class and used as a video-enhanced lecture. The professor used a PowerMac 6100 as a projector with an LCD Active Matrix Panel, and the students clearly understood the relationships of the overall lecture outline and the examples. Copies of the individual screens and lecture notes were printed and made available to the students, another feature that they appreciated.

Guidelines

1. Consider the steps of the program development when creating original multimedia programs—specialized instructional design, programming and mastering, computer programming, development of needed documentation, and evaluation are necessary.

2. Make certain that the roles needed in original development—manager, instructional designers, production experts, computer programmers, and evaluators are fulfilled.

3. Of special importance is an understanding of the nature of gross and Level Two flowcharting, of the process of creating storyboards, of knowing the steps in production and editing, and of working with computer programmers if a Level Three application formal instructional program is desired.

4. Formative evaluation and beta testing takes on particular importance when the computer program is added to the multimedia application—does all the branching work properly? Do the sequences made sense? A design team with different roles is vital if an original application needs to be created.

Resources

Pioneers in developing resource materials for original creation of multimedia programs were DeBloois and Iuppa who, in the early and mid 1980s developed guidelines for the process, from detailed support for flowcharting and story-boarding to suggestions for production and programming. These guidelines remain relevant today.

Dick and Carey (1985) have outlined a systematic process for the design of instruction, which includes identifying an instructional goal, conducting instructional analysis of a goal, and instructional analysis of subordinate skills in designing and conducting formative and summative evaluations.

Bergman and Moore (1990) include in-depth consideration of orientation issues, preparation of the project, construction of the multimedia program, and implementation and management. They provide numerous checklists for evaluating each phase of the project, storyboard formats, and ideas for writing a grant proposal to secure funding. Their work is a vital resource for anyone undertaking an original application.

Two other books provide contemporary perspectives on developing multimedia applications. Vaughan (1993) provides background information and guidelines on how to design and build multimedia applications from the ground up. Wolfgram (1994) covers numerous aspects of creating multimedia applications.

Journals such as *Educational Technology, Educational Technology Research and Development, Educational Technology Systems,* and *Technological Horizons in Education (T. H. E. Journal)* provide articles that describe various aspects of development. Journals related to one's professional field sometimes contain helpful articles.

One of the most useful resources are preconference tutorials provided by the Society for Applied Learning Technology (SALT). Sessions usually address the design, development, and management of multimedia creation. Often they provide tutorials related to specific instructional design formats such as simulations or tutorials. The training sessions at the University of Nebraska— Lincoln provide the simulated creation of an original program.

Internet connections with other developers around the world can provide immediate answers as questions arise during the original development. Many campuses now have easily accessible connections for databases and electronic bulletin boards; media or library specialists can provide needed information.

Conclusion

The roles of manager, instructional designers, production experts, computer programmers, and evaluators are necessary for successful completion of projects. The instructional design, production, computer programming, and formative evaluation are long and arduous tasks. In our development of original programs, we failed at first to recognize the tedious and precise nature of completing Level Two flowcharts and storyboards, and we underestimated the time needed for production and the beta testing aspects of formative evaluation. These tasks must be adequately accounted for in the personnel budget.

When students work with new platforms to produce their own original multimedia programs, the steps outlined, although done in a more informal and interactive manner, must still be completed. The students must be provided adequate laboratories, staffed with laboratory assistants who are familiar with the latest multimedia technologies.

Developing an original application to meet an educational problem is a time-consuming and often expensive alternative. The time and money are well spent, nonetheless, when it results in the exact application needed to solve an educational problem.

CHAPTER 8

GENERATING SOLUTIONS: REPURPOSING MULTIMEDIA APPLICATIONS

Goals

Repurposing multimedia applications refers to using videodiscs, CD-ROMs, or other multimedia elements that have been completed by others to generate a new instructional design. The process involves development of a computer program to tailor, or repurpose, the existing applications to more effectively address the educational problem you have identified. Repurposing provides a middle ground between obtaining an off-the-shelf application developed elsewhere and creating your own application "from scratch."

The repurposing activity incorporates the basic problem solving process used in developing and using multimedia in general. This book has already described several aspects of this process, such as defining the educational problem, reviewing multimedia hardware and its capabilities, and examining possible instructional models and methods of use. Repurposing involves building on this process to identify appropriate existing multimedia elements and to organize them into coherent applications. Two key aspects require further elaboration: (1) developing a specialized instructional design associated with repurposing, and (2) completing a computer program to coordinate the various multimedia elements and allowing for appropriate interactivity. This chapter, therefore, focuses on the general process to be used in multimedia repurposing and, in particular, on the specialized instructional design and programming activities associated with repurposing. This process has been developed previously by Falk (1993).

General Information

Most traditional instructional design processes for developing your own Level Three videodisc or multimedia applications begin with defining the educational problem and proceed to specifying an overall instructional design, developing a general flowchart, and writing scripts and storyboards. The computer program is written at about the same time as production occurs. Only at the very end of this process, after post-production and mastering, does the videodisc, CD-ROM, or other form of multimedia application itself become available (see Chapter 7).

Repurposing can start concurrently at either end of this traditional sequence and gradually work its way toward the middle through an interactive process. One may find a videodisc and recognize its significant potential to address a familiar educational problem; conversely one may first identify an educational problem and then find a videodisc and/or other multimedia elements that could address that need. One way or another, the instructional designer must "bridge the gap" between the educational problem and the existing multimedia material through instructional design and computer programming. The interactive process of multimedia repurposing is described below. This process includes several general steps and decision points (see Figure 8.1).

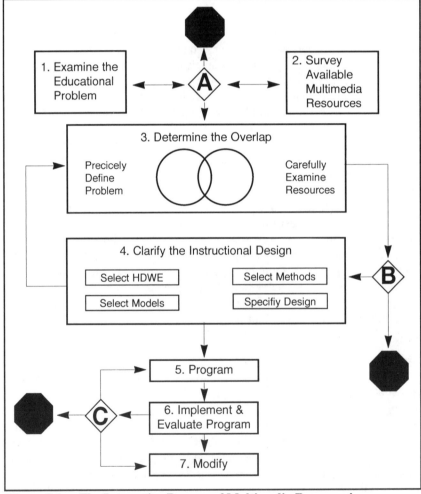

Figure 8.1   **The Interactive Process of Multimedia Repurposing**

Step 1: Review the Educational Problem

The first step of repurposing remains the same as most instructional design processes. It is important, in a general way, to review the instructional goals and objectives and other aspects of defining the educational problem. In actuality, this step may be stimulated by identifying a videodisc or other multimedia resource that may have potential teaching or learning advantages, but it is important that you define the general instructional goal and educational problem before examining available multimedia in greater depth.

Step 2: Survey Available Videodiscs and Other Multimedia Resources

The number and range of videodisc, CD-ROM, and other multimedia applications are growing rapidly. Chapter 6 provided examples of a number of resources that can be acquired and put to immediate use. Any elements of these existing applications might also be incorporated into a repurposed multimedia application. Most of the same sources for multimedia applications listed in Chapter 6 also distribute generic or Level One videodiscs that can be programmed to address specific educational problems and to meet particular learning needs. Other multimedia resources that could be integrated into an existing application include clip art, sound and audio, animation, graphics, and scanned images.

The key activity in this step is to locate multimedia elements that may address the educational problem previously identified and to collect sufficient information about them to determine whether they have the potential to meet the instructional goals and objectives. Upon such determination, you have reached the first decision point.

Decision point A. If no videodiscs or other multimedia resources exist that may reasonably be expected to meet the identified educational problem, you can return to the teaching/learning situation and seek other ways to improve instruction; or, assuming that your campus has the necessary resources, you can develop your own multimedia application. If you find relevant applications, you can more carefully and precisely define the educational problem and then examine those products to determine which, if any, seems amenable to repurposing.

Step 3: Determining the Overlap Between the Educational Problem and the Multimedia Resources

Step 3a: More precisely define the problem. Having identified the general content area of available multimedia resources, the designer can focus on the learning needs and outcomes that could be met using these resources. Specific learner characteristics and learning objectives are developed. The key issue is to further clarify and delineate the educational problem that may be better met using the identified multimedia resources.

Step 3b: Carefully examine the multimedia resources. After defining the educational problem more clearly, you should carefully examine the specific content of the various relevant multimedia resources. What specific motion sequences, still images, and audio can be used from a videodisc? What data or images can be used from a CD-ROM? What digitized graphics, clip art, or animation can be incorporated? What other video, audio, or graphics exist in digitized form or could be readily and legally converted to a digitized form?

The key task here is to identify the exact multimedia elements that could be incorporated into an application and to record their precise location. For example, if a relevant videodisc exists, one would identify, locate (i.e., by frame numbers), and list those portions that are usable.

Decision point B. After a more rigorous examination of the educational problem and the available multimedia resources, it is again important to determine whether repurposing makes sense. The key question: At this point does it seem that the anticipated improvement in learning that may result from using these multimedia resources is worth the time, the effort, and the cost required to develop the repurposed application? A negative answer means you can cut losses and put energies into other instructional strategies. If affirmative, one can proceed to clarify the specialized instructional design for repurposing.

Step 4: Clarify the Instructional Design

Specifying the instructional design includes taking advantage of and working within the limitations of the available multimedia hardware, determining the instructional use(s) and model(s), and specifying the exact nature of the instruction. Each of these aspects of the design process is described below.

Step 4a: Examine appropriate/available hardware. Numerous hardware options exist (see Chapter 4). Each platform or system offers different features and limitations that must be taken into account. On the one hand, the instructional design for the repurposed application should fully employ the capabilities of the hardware that furthers the achievement of the instructional goals and objectives; on the other hand, it is important to design within parameters determined by the available hardware. If you have a powerful development system capable of digitizing video and audio and a number of delivery systems available for student use, almost any multimedia resource can be incorporated into a repurposed application. If you have only a basic computer and videodisc player that serves as both a development and a delivery system for teaching a larger class, you must use only portions of the videodisc application as a teaching tool.

Step 4b: Select the method(s) of use. Multimedia applications can be used as either a teaching tool or a learning tool (see Chapter 5). An application can be used as a teaching tool with the teacher or trainer selectively augmenting classroom instruction with motion sequences, stills, and audio from the application in the classroom setting. An application can also be used as a learning tool with an individual learner sitting at a videodisc workstation and completing an interactive, individualized, self-paced application. The repurposed application can also be designed for use as both a teaching and a learning tool.

The choice of instructional mode affects the hardware requirements and specificity of programming required. An instructor needs only a single multimedia system to use the application as a teaching tool; more systems are required for use as a learning tool, particularly with large classes. In general, repurposing multimedia for use as a teaching tool is much easier because only one individual, the instructor, must navigate through the program. Also, the developer (who could, in fact, also be the user), does not need to be as complete and specific in preparing operating instructions.

Step 4c: Select specific instructional model(s). Many instructional or learning activities are also available, regardless of the method of use selected (see Chapter 5). Video-enhanced didactic presentations, exploration, case studies, simulated interaction, and assessment and focused instruction represent instructional models that may be incorporated into the repurposed application. The key task is to select the instructional model(s) that make best use of the multimedia resources to achieve the identified goals with learners who have the characteristics identified above.

Step 4d: Specify the instructional design. Once you have identified the instructional mode and learning activities, you should, in some way, specify the instructional design. Possible methods include flowcharting the movement through the application, scripting the computer text, and/or storyboarding to clarify both the computer text and graphics and the design flow. Actually, the designer may be able to assemble the instructional design along the way by combining (1) a clear knowledge of the learner needs and objectives, (2) clearly identified multimedia resources, and (3) thorough knowledge and use of flexible software.

Step 5: Programming the Repurposed Application

Once you have clarified the instructional design, the next step involves writing the software. A number of programming options are reviewed below. We also describe the activities involved in actually undertaking the programming.

Step 5a: Selecting programming software. Numerous software options exist for most hardware platforms. Because the chapter on hardware focused on Apple Macintosh and IBM and compatible multimedia platforms, this section provides examples of authoring systems that can be used with these two types of platforms. These same authoring possibilities relate to programming applications that are developed from scratch (see Chapter 7).

Several criteria are relevant when examining possible software packages for use in programming a multimedia application. These considerations include ease of use; opportunities for student evaluation options such as multiple choice and fill-in-the-blank questions; consistency of interface; possibility of full integration of graphics, text, animation, sound, and video; presence of drivers for various videodisc players; integration of external applications; hypertext functions; availability of interactive graphics; color text and graphics capabilities; ability to print materials from the application; ability to transport, land, and return within any section of the application; software access to laserdisc player character (text) overlay; digital video capabilities; ability to use digital sound; animation capabilities; graphic overlay capabilities; support for single-screen presentation; special effects capabilities; and last, but certainly not least, cost (Anderson & Veljkov, 1990).

A number of authoring systems exist for Macintosh platforms, including HyperCard, Aldus SuperCard, Action, Passport Producer, MacroMind Director, Course Builder, Test Factory, Apple Media Tool, and Authorware Professional. Some of these packages are reviewed briefly below, but remember that their producers continuously change and evolve them through different versions.

HyperCard. Sometimes described as a "software erector set," HyperCard is a low-cost ($199 list) application that can control videodisc players, CD-ROMs, and VCRs through the use of external commands (XCMDs). HyperCard's strengths include its relative ease of use for beginners and nonprofessionals on simple projects, ease of using QuickTime movies, and ability to create simple projects quickly and to expand. Limitations include lack of integrated graphics, animation tools, and color.

Action. Action is Macromedia's entry-level package ($495 list) and provides powerful media integration tools and sufficient flexibility to create a variety of multimedia presentations. It is primarily designed for those who have used slide presentation software and now want to add multimedia elements. This application allows the programmer to create a series of scenes to which graphics, text, movies, sound objects, QuickTime files, and other multimedia elements can be added simultaneously or consecutively.

Authorware Professional. This application represents a more expensive ($2,000 list for educational users) program that incorporates icons and dialog boxes rather than a scripting language. Its strengths include extensive built-in media integration, ease of handling color, excellent animation tools, extensive testing options and student tracking capabilities, and a Windows version that makes cross-platform development fairly straightforward. Limitations include a steep learning curve and cost.

Other Macintosh authoring software. Numerous other software options exist for the Macintosh. Aldus SuperCard takes the same approach as HyperCard, but adds color and better animation controls with a similarly low cost ($299 list). MacroMind Director provides excellent controls over animations and is a very good tool for presentations. Test Factory from Warren-Forethought provides testing and tracking for one-half the cost ($939 list) of Authorware, but its use is difficult to learn.

Authoring software packages for IBM and compatible platforms include LinkWay, TenCORE, Quest, Guide, Multimedia Toolbook, IconAuthor, and Authorware Professional for Windows. Three of these options are briefly described below (Anderson & Veljkov, 1990; Poor, 1992).

Linkway. This application is an IBM version of Macintosh's HyperCard, providing low-cost access to multimedia authoring in an easy-to-use format. Linkway allows the user to graphically create screens and buttons that link multiple pieces of information from a variety of multimedia sources.

Multimedia Toolbook. In some ways, this application also emulates HyperCard, and serves as the tool of choice in the Windows environment for many who want to create hypertext-like documents with integrated multimedia elements. It incorporates a book metaphor and includes a variety of tools that can be accessed readily if one takes the time to master their use. Toolbook includes a variety of features at a relatively low cost ($695 list).

Authorware Professional for Windows. The Windows version has a flow-chart interface and extensive features, along with advantages and disadvantages similar to the version available for the Macintosh (see above). It represents a sound choice for programming sophisticated applications that use Multimedia Extensions. The listed cost is $2,000 for educational users.

Other IBM authoring software. The Multimedia Development Kit for Microsoft can add multimedia capabilities to existing Windows applications for a relatively low cost ($595 list). Quest, from Allen Communications, is a popu-lar and widely used authoring system that has evolved over the years, but still allows multimedia programming without fancy and expensive hardware. IconAuthor from AimTech provides a flowchart-based interface with several tools that are easy to use but that can become unwieldy in large productions.

Step 5b: Complete computer programming. Once you have selected the soft-ware, it is now necessary to actually program the computer in accordance with the specified instructional design. The process can be time consuming and tedious; however, the application's smooth and efficient operation depends on the successful completion of this step.

In general terms, the programming involves creating and organizing all of the elements of the multimedia application (text, graphics, video, animation, audio, etc.) and linking them to create a seamless presentation that either the teacher or the learners control. A key decision is whether the instructor writes her or his own software programs. For a small project requiring less sophisticated multi-media elements and links, an instructor knowledgeable about a particular appli-cation may be able to manage quite well. A larger, more complex project will probably require a professional programmer.

Decision point C. At several times during Steps 4 and 5, the designer may again ask whether repurposing the selected disc is worth the effort it (in essence, a continuation of decision point B). The answer may well be no if appropriate equipment is not available, the time required for programming is too extensive, or the appropriate instructional designs do not emerge. If the designer decides to abandon the project, at least he or she will have learned something and will be better prepared to repurpose (or choose not to do so) in the future. If Steps 4 and 5 are completed, the designer is ready to move on.

Step 6: Implement and Evaluate the Application

After beta testing or otherwise completing a preliminary check on the func-tioning of the repurposed application, you should be ready to try it out with those learners for whose benefit it is intended. The test may involve using the applica-tion as a teaching tool to enhance a classroom presentation, providing self-paced, individualized instruction for students outside of class, or any one of myriad possibilities (see Chapter 10).

It is important that you determine whether the repurposed application is effective in meeting the previously identified learner needs. Does the application result in increased knowledge or enhanced skills? What do the learners think about this new technology? Do they perceive it as valuable and worthwhile? What are the strengths and limitations of the application as it currently exists? How could it be improved? (See Chapter 11.)

Decision point D. Based on the evaluation results, several actions could follow. In the worst case scenario, the application fails dismally in terms of learner outcomes and satisfaction. The program should be erased from your hard disc and banished forever. Fortunately, that rarely happens. In the best case, the application brought outstanding learning outcomes and universal satisfaction, in which case you can rest on your laurels until the next opportunity to use the application arises. Most often the evaluation provides results somewhere between these two extremes, indicating an opportunity to further refine the repurposed application to bring it closer to the ideal product envisioned.

Questions

The following questions provide guidance for repurposing multimedia applications.

1. What is the nature of the educational problem that could be addressed with multimedia? What are the instructional goals and objectives? What are the characteristics of the learners?
2. What multimedia resources are available to address the educational problem identified?
    — Videodiscs?
    — CD-ROMs?
    — Video that can be easily and legally digitized?
    — Clip art?
    — Other digitized graphics?
    — Scanned images?
    — Digitized audio/sound resources?
    — Sounds/audio that can be easily and legally digitized?
    — Animation?
3. Do sufficient multimedia resources exist to support repurposing as a way to address the educational problem?
4. What hardware would be necessary to use the repurposed application? Is it available?
5. What method of use (teaching tool or learning tool) would be appropriate for this repurposed application?
6. What instructional design(s) can most effectively combine the multimedia elements into an effective application?

— Video-enhanced didactic presentations?
— Exploration?
— Structured observation?
— Simulated personal interaction?
— Assessment and focused instruction?
— Other models?

7. What computer programming resources will facilitate development of the repurposed application?

8. Does this application represent a more cost-effective alternative than other learning options (see Chapter 9)? If so, how should the application be implemented (see Chapter 10) and evaluated (see Chapter 11)?

Examples

Example One: Human Development

The first case example is based on a relatively simple repurposing effort that identified a single existing videodisc and then selectively used a portion of the videodisc to develop a repurposed application. This application was completed several years ago.

Step 1: Reviewing the educational problem and *Step 2: Surveying multimedia resources.* In February 1990 the author was preparing to teach a course on human development and had developed some general instructional goals for the course (Step 1). That same month he attended the SALT conference in Orlando and heard about a generic videodisc on psychology that had recently been developed by Scott Foresman & Company (Step 2). A general description of the disc indicated that some of the material might be helpful in achieving some of the course's performance objectives, so the author decided to obtain the try to repurpose the disc for use in the human development course (decision point A).

Step 3: Determining overlap between the educational problem and multimedia resources. When *The Psychology Encyclopedia* videodisc arrived, the author had already begun teaching the human development course and had more clearly specified performance objectives, including that students know prominent developmental psychologists and their theories and that they understand the dynamics of prenatal development (Step 3a). He then carefully reviewed the videodisc content, aided by its complete and accurate content documentation, and he identified numerous specific stills and motion segments that could be useful in achieving the objectives (Step 3b). While the videodisc could have been used in the Level 1 format with a keypad, the author's desire for greater interactivity and distaste for fumbling around with a keypad led to a decision to proceed with repurposing (decision point B).

Step 4: Clarifying the instructional design. Several activities were involved in this step. Initially, the author examined available hardware. He decided that a Macintosh SE computer, a Pioneer 6000 videodisc player, and a television monitor would function as the delivery system because they possessed the necessary capabilities and were readily available (Step 4a). Because of the limited hardware available, the author decided to use the multimedia application as a teaching tool in an upcoming class session (Step 4b). He further decided to use the stills and motion sequences as resources to enhance didactic presentations on theories of human development and on prenatal development (Step 4c). The instructional design was specified in the author's mind (Step 4d), and it included still images from the videodisc of various theorists to provide visual introductions of the people involved, motion sequences to demonstrate key concepts, and graphics to clarify certain relationships.

Step 5: Programming the repurposed application. HyperCard software was chosen as the authoring system because it was suitable for the instructional needs and the author knew how to use it (Step 5a). A relatively simple HyperCard stack was developed to access the desired stills, video, and audio from the videodisc (Step 5b). The actual programming involved creating a stack of about thirty cards, linking still images from the videodisc to specific cards so the image from the disc would be displayed on the TV monitor when the card appeared on the computer screen, and creating buttons that would activate a specific video motion sequence when required.

Step 6: Implementing and evaluating the application. After reviewing the application that had been developed, the author decided to use the repurposed videodisc in the human development class (decision point C). It should be noted that about ten hours of work had gone into developing this repurposed application. As implemented, the application included (1) showing pictures of the theorists as their names were mentioned, (2) presenting video examples of concepts such as conservation of volume and classical and operant conditioning, and (3) showing about twenty stills of prenatal development, first in chronological order and then randomly to demonstrate the development of various body parts.

The repurposed application was evaluated by examining student performance on the subsequent test items that addressed the concepts and information included in the application and by completing a brief satisfaction survey. An item analysis indicated that the students scored well on the test material covered by the videodisc application. The satisfaction survey indicated that the portion of the class incorporating videodisc material received an average rating of 6.5 on a scale ranging from 1 ("not at all valuable") to 7 ("very valuable").

Based on the student evaluation, the repurposed application was used in subsequent courses (decision point D). The application was also modified based on feedback received during the evaluation process.

Example Two: Information on American Indians

This case example describes a repurposing activity that is currently in process on the University of Minnesota, Duluth campus. It involves digitizing existing resources and integrating them into a repurposed application that students can use as a learning tool outside of class.

Step 1: Reviewing the educational problem and *Step 2: Surveying multimedia resources.* The author recently developed a new course on race, class, and gender in the United States. Included in the general instructional goals for the course are that students come to (1) understand the historical background of different races and the cultural differences that may exist among them, and (2) know some of the contributions that different races have made to the United States (Step 1). The author was also aware of a videodisc on campus that covered aspects of life related to Ojibwe Indians and a CD-ROM on American Indians (Step 2). The author knew much of the videodisc's content well, and a general description of the CD-ROM indicated that some of the material on this disc might be helpful in achieving some of the course's goals. The author decided to obtain the videodisc and CD-ROM and review the content of these resources (decision point A).

Step 3: Determining overlap between the educational problem and multimedia resources. The goals for the course related to American Indians were more precisely defined at this point. These goals included that students would be able to (1) describe specific treaties and laws and how they affected American Indians, (2) describe the philosophies and specific medicinal cures related to Indian health practices, and (3) explain several contributions that Indian nations had made to the United States (Step 3a).

The contents of the videodisc and of the CD-ROM were explored and numerous examples of text, specific stills, and motion segments that could be useful in achieving the objectives were identified. Other resources, such as graphics that could be scanned, text from on-line sources that could be copied, and existing digitized graphics were also identified (Step 3b).

At this point, the professor determined that considerable overlap existed between the more specific goals for the course and the multimedia resources that were available. A decision to go forward with the repurposing activities was therefore made (decision point B).

Step 4: Clarifying the instructional design. After the author examined available hardware, it was decided that Macintosh IIci computers would be used as both the development and delivery system for the repurposed application. Implicit in this decision was the understanding that all of the material would be digitized, so that no peripheral devices such as videodisc players or CD-ROM drives would be required. An MPC platform could have served the hardware needs equally well in this situation (Step 4a).

The author decided to use the repurposed multimedia application as a learning tool for students to use outside of the classroom. Several computer laboratories on campus possessed sufficient Macintosh equipment for the students to access and use as they would choose (Step 4b). The author also decided to use exploration as the primary instructional model, allowing students to move through the options as they wished and to achieve the goals of the application in a variety of ways (Step 4c).

A general flowchart of the instructional design was prepared to guide the programming and the selection of resources from the videodisc, CD-ROM, and other sources. The flowchart indicated that students would be able to explore a variety of content related to history, culture, and contributions, and that the design incorporated hypertext, numerous still images, audio that included the Ojibwe language and music, and some full-motion video (Step 4d).

Step 5: Programming the repurposed application. HyperCard was again chosen as the authoring system. The product's low cost and ease of use were again important considerations; HyperCard also allows hypertext capabilities and the ability to incorporate a variety of multimedia options, including full-motion video from QuickTime (step 5a).

The actual programming is now underway and will result in an extensive HyperCard stack or, perhaps, collection of stacks. The methodology involves importing text from the CD-ROM and from an online collection of historical documents. One imported document is the constitution of the Iroquois Confederacy, many aspects of which were incorporated into the U.S. Constitution. Other text describes numerous aspects of Indian history and of the different Indian nations. The digitized audio (imported with MacRecorder) includes several dialogues and numerous words from the Ojibwe language and a sampling of traditional Ojibwe music. The still images and full-motion video are imported into QuickTime and include a simulated video interview with a traditional Indian medicine man, stills of plants used in traditional medicines, and stills of the original treaties and laws affecting American Indians to this day. Scanned images of Indian art and symbols have been imported (after checking with Indian consultants for appropriateness) and provide attractive graphics throughout the application (Step 5b).

Step 6: Implementing and evaluating the application. The application is currently being completed and will be used in the initial offering of the race, class, and gender course during the next academic year. Students will be provided with questions to guide their exploration of the multimedia application, focusing their attention on the goals that the instructor has for this particular section of the course. Students will also be asked to evaluate their experience with the multimedia application, including an overall rating of the value of the instruction, information on what aspects of the multimedia instruction were most effective, and ideas about how the application could be improved.

Guidelines

1. As usual, begin the process of repurposing with the educational problem clearly in mind.
2. Explore possible multimedia resources, including videodiscs and CD-ROM, to identify elements that could be used in a repurposed application.

3. Define the instructional goals and learner characteristics more precisely and explore the resources more carefully to identify overlap. Videodiscs in particular are easier to explore if a thorough index is included.

4. If sufficient overlap exists, clarify the instructional design by (1) selecting the hardware to be used, (2) determining the method(s) of use, (3) identifying the instructional model(s) to be incorporated, and (4) specifying the design in preparation for computer programming. In general, it is easier to develop an application for use as a teaching tool.

5. Select an appropriate authoring system and complete the programming. Numerous options exist, many of which are relatively inexpensive and easy to use.

6. Implement and evaluate the repurposed application. Be prepared to modify the application based on the feedback received.

7. Throughout the repurposing process, attend to copyright issues when using multimedia elements from other sources. In general, if the material does not provide permission to copy, it is necessary to seek authorization from the copyright holder.

Resources

Key resources include the multimedia elements that go into the repurposed application. The "Resources" section of Chapter 6 identifies sources for videodiscs and CD-ROMs. As a brief summary, the *Videodisc Compendium* from Emerging Technology Consultants and *CD-ROMs in Print* from Mecklermedia are valuable sources of titles in these areas.

Other multimedia resources include digital video, digitized sound, clip art, and animation clips. These resources are often described in periodicals related to specific computers (e.g., *MacUser* and *PC World*) and can be obtained through computer catalogs (e.g., *MacConnection* and *Tiger Software*). Information concerning legal issues related to using multimedia elements produced by others can be obtained from MacIntosh (1990).

The capabilities, advantages, and disadvantages of authoring systems appropriate for multimedia are regularly described in periodical articles. For example, *PC Magazine* described three authoring systems in its March 31, 1992 issue and *MacWorld* reviewed a number of systems in the March 1993 issue. Sales (1989), Arch (1994), and Barron and Baumbach (1990) provide information about authoring tools for repurposing, and Sayre and Montgomery (1990) and Falk (1991, 1993) write specifically about repurposing.

It is quite possible to obtain information about authoring systems directly from the vendors. The names and telephone numbers of the vendors mentioned in the general information earlier in this chapter appear in the appendix of this book. Authoring system vendors are also frequent exhibitors at many of the conferences sponsored by the organizations listed in the appendix.

Conclusion

Repurposing represents a promising middle ground between using an existing multimedia application and developing your own complete application. By repurposing, you gain the advantage of tailoring an application to your specific needs; and, compared to the production costs involved in making your own application, repurposing is relatively inexpensive.

Like most other aspects of multimedia in higher education, the best way to learn about repurposing is to try it—either individually or with a team. By starting small with a single resource such as a videodisc and a relatively simple authoring system such as HyperCard, you can develop an application for use as a teaching tool with a limited expenditure of time and money. Alternatively, you can begin with presentation software such as Aldus Persuasion or Microsoft PowerPoint and add QuickTime sequences that include video and audio components. Once you begin, a wide range of opportunities will open for you.

PART 3

Selecting, Using, and Evaluating Multimedia

Part 1 emphasized the importance of carefully defining the educational problem to be addressed, and Part 2 described multimedia as a set of solutions with the potential to address a variety of educational problems. Now, Part 3 focuses on the decision whether to use multimedia to solve a particular educational problem and on implementing and evaluating multimedia solutions if they are selected.

Chapter 9 describes a number of criteria to consider in examining the advantages and disadvantages of multimedia as an instructional tool. These criteria include (1) the match between the model of instruction, method of use, and educational problem, (2) the quality of the instructional design, and (3) the technical quality of the application.

Chapter 10 explains considerations in implementing or using a multimedia application after it has been selected as the best solution to an educational problem. Fostering interactivity is a key component of using multimedia applications. It is important to rehearse prior to use. Guidelines for using multimedia as a learning tool or as a teaching tool are provided.

Chapter 11 provides information about evaluating the development and use of multimedia. Formative evaluation involves collecting information that will assist in improving the quality of the multimedia application and its use; this type of evaluation can occur throughout the problem solving process. Summative evaluation focuses on assessing the effectiveness of the multimedia application, either in terms of achieving the goals of the instruction or of assessing the effectiveness of multimedia compared to other forms of instruction. Relevant variables for consideration are proposed.

As in Parts 1 and 2, the chapters in Part 3 begin with goals and proceed to a general background on the topic. Relevant questions are proposed and case examples described. Guidelines related to the topic and resources for further exploration precede the summary and conclusion in each chapter.

CHAPTER 9

DECIDING AMONG ALTERNATIVES: THE NICHE FOR MULTIMEDIA

Goals

After you have defined the educational problem and explored the various multimedia solutions, you should then examine the alternative solutions available and select a solution for implementation. This involves systematically developing and using criteria to determine (1) which instructional model will be used; (2) whether multimedia is a viable instructional tool for the instructional model selected; (3) which multimedia resource is needed to meet requirements of the instructional model selected; (4) whether the quality of the instructional design is adequate; (5) whether the technical quality of the multimedia program is adequate; and (6) whether the necessary hardware is immediately available or readily accessible. In short, one needs to determine whether multimedia occupies a niche to address a particular educational problem and to specify the nature of that niche.

General Information

Criteria for the Selection of an Instructional Model

Various options for engaging in the instructional process are outlined in Chapter 5. Those options include video-enhanced didactic presentations, exploration, structured observation, simulated personal interaction, and assessment and focused instruction. In turn these models can be used as either teaching tools or learning tools with individual students, small groups, or large groups.

To determine which model to use, the professor needs to consider the broad goals of instruction at the university level discussed previously: impart knowledge, encourage critical thinking and problem solving, develop appreciation for cultural diversity, teach how to use the key processes for analysis and collecting evidence in various fields, and prepare students for effective job performance. If the professor's goal is to impart knowledge, the video-enhanced didactic presentation model could be appropriate. On the other hand, if the goal is process oriented and focused on cultural diversity, an exploration or a simulated personal interaction model could be used.

After addressing the general goals, the professor needs to review course goals and learning objectives for specific classes and assignments. These goals and objectives should mesh with the broad goals of higher education.

Next, the learner characteristics need to be understood. Gender, ability, age, ethnicity, developmental needs, and learning style are among the characteristics that must be understood and accommodated. Multimedia applications with optional learning tracks can be designed for differing learner charactristics. For example, offering two optional tracks, exploration or assessment and focused instruction, can accommodate different learning styles..

Criteria for the Selection of Appropriate Instructional Tools

Once you have selected the instructional model, you must next consider whether multimedia or other instructional tools should be used. When compared with other instructional tools, multimedia should be used if learners need to "interact" with the media; for example, if the professor desires that nothing happens until a student or group of students makes a response, then multimedia could be more useful than textbooks. The need to have quick and easy access to material for multiple observations and comparisons through rapid random access is also an important consideration in selecting multimedia. Finally, if personalized visual learning sequences need to be used, either as an instructional program for individual learners or as a database for learner-created visual essays, multimedia offers unique solutions.

Multimedia is also useful if moving video or stills are needed as concrete examples for observation and analysis. Particularly important is access to "remote" occurrences—events from other times and places. Concrete examples that offer common referents for discussion are also important.

Multimedia should not be selected merely to provide a talking head lecture by a professor of the same status, culture, and background as the course instructor. Abstract concepts are better presented without the use of multimedia.

In summary, it is important that you consider the unique characteristics of multimedia. These characteristics can help determine whether multimedia fills the niche needed to provide a solution for a particular educational problem.

Criteria for Evaluating the Design of Instruction

Good multimedia educational materials take advantage of the medium's unique capabilities. Programs can enable a student to both master a body of knowledge and engage with peers in problem solving. Unfortunately, not all materials available and marketed are of high quality. Instructors must properly evaluate software and hardware to make informed choices. Otherwise, they might simply buy blindly or follow the most heavily marketed and latest fad.

Scott, Cole, and Engel (1992) identified some considerations for evaluating choices in selecting software. Both the level of learner/computer interaction and the level of cognitive/mental thinking must be considered when choosing multimedia programs. Is the program's use that of drill and practice, tutorial instruction, instructional games, simulation, problem solving, spreadsheets, word processing, or database management? Are gender and ethnicity sensitively portrayed?

Raitt (1989) and Barron & Baumbach (1990) discussed selection guidelines for CD-ROM. They recommend that purchasers of CD-ROM titles consider the instructional design, the combinations of materials available on the disc, the product's testing, the workstation configurations necessary to use the software, and the cost of the program related to its benefits. Rendell (1991) suggests questions to consider when moving into the use of instructional technology such as CD-ROM: Why should I? What hardware should I choose? Where do I start? What software should I buy? What problems or pitfalls might I encounter? Particularly important are considerations of the purposes for use of new technologies, such as word processing, information retrieval, simulations, text manipulations, or language work. Anticipating problems such as disk management, time management and scheduling, authoring problems, and output options also are important.

Riskin (1990), in his discussion of an experimental, nontraditional university class in sociology, suggests that professors consider the various aspects of hypermedia and their effects on student learning. For example, the interactivity available on multimedia should promote nonlinear creative thinking among students so that an objective structure grows out of a subjective mass of material. Use of multimedia should help students span the gap between two forms of knowledge—personal creative reasoning and the objective world of social phenomena.

Tucker and Dempsey (1991) suggest several important criteria in evaluating and selecting hypermedia. Because students have the opportunity to manage information, professors need to consider how the text is linked to both the student and to the audience for which the student is developing a particular project; they need to be aware that a decentering and recentering process exists in which students make their own interests the center of learning rather than follow a predetermined program developed by an absent author. Professors also must consider how to mediate the networking and navigation of individuals developing their own learning paths through masses of material available on CD-ROM or interactive videodiscs. Also important are the boundaries of projects in which there are possibilities for nonsequential reading and thinking and where differences may exist between novice and expert knowledge representations.

Sloane, Gordon, Gunn, and Michelsen (1989) identified the following types of questions in the educational software evaluation process: (1) What can the software program do that other instructional tools can't? (2) Will the software run on my hardware system? (3) Will it meet my instructional goals? (4) Is the instructional design effective? (5) Is the program technically well-designed? (6) Does the program have management features? (7) Is the documentation complete and easy to use? (8) Has the program been evaluated for its instructional effectiveness; that is, how well has it been shown to teach what it is supposed to teach?

Thus, after the professor chooses the teaching-learning model and decides to use multimedia, the next step involves locating, developing, or repurposing various programs. As these programs are reviewed, it is important to use appropriate criteria in analyzing the quality of their instructional design. Some criteria are applicable to all formats of programs; others apply to specific formats. Effective instructional designs include appropriate meta messages—examples chosen are ethnically and gender sensitive; and some examples promote a transformed society. Good instructional designs, whether for CD-ROM, DVI, or CD-I, contain clear goals, specific directions for use or access, appropriate feedback, the ability to review material when necessary, and adequate time for learning. Easily accessed and understandable help screens should be available. Particularly important are directions to access previous screens or to move to the next screen. The cost must be reasonable—usually it is less expensive to purchase an already developed program than to develop original programs. Learners should enjoy using the program and find it helpful in learning important concepts.

In addition to these general criteria for selection, specific criteria address different formats. For example, in developing a Level One videodisc/CD ROM program for explorative use by an individual (either student or professorial), small group, or large group, it is most important to understand the overall organization of the multimedia software. Often the material includes a printed "table of contents." Knowing how to use the bar code or remote control devices to access the information is also vital, as are ways to compile the program information.

If the Level Three videodisc/CD-ROM program is developed for assessment and focused instruction, learner control of the pace and sequence of instruction is needed. Tests appropriate to the content being taught should be included. Remedial loops should offer alternative instruction, not mere repetition of original instruction. The ability to use the materials independently with appropriate manuals and other documentation is essential.

If the Level Three program is designed for group use, it is helpful if it provides appropriate directions and discussion points. The content should be amenable to group discussion—a simulation or problem solving multimedia program would be helpful.

Criteria for Determining Technical Quality

Criteria for determining the technical quality of multimedia have been discussed, in part, by Schmidt (1992). Among the criteria are those related to (1) organization (use of introduction and summaries), (2) picture and sound (quality of lighting, fades, color, music, special effects, known cues to understand unknown features, side-by-side multiple images), (3) overall characteristics (dramatic sequences with exceptional acting, message adequately developed through fades, dissolves, superimpositions, zooms), and (4) editing (cuts and short changes synchronized with music; satisfying shot order, dissolves used to disguise jump cuts).

In addition, the following items should be considered to determine the technical quality. First, it is important for learners that the overall and help instructions are clearly presented. A logical and orderly presentation facilitates users' comprehension. Varieties of displays and response modes assist the learner. Realistic examples, with superb acting and sets that are motivating, enhance learning. Graphics, color, and sound that are consistent and highlight important points are useful. Editing with dissolves combining different types of shots in a smooth way is important. Easy-to-read text with consistent formats aid the learner. Finally, hardware that runs reliably is crucial to the learner's continued involvement.

Questions

To apply the above general criteria for examining alternatives and selecting a solution to a particular situation, the following questions can be asked:

1. Which instructional model (video-enhanced didactic presentation, exploration, structured observation, simulated personal interaction, assessment and focused instruction) should I select?

   Which model is most consistent with the broad goals I consider important for higher education?

   Which model is most consistent with my course goals and lesson objectives?

   Which model most readily meets the needs of my students?

2. Is multimedia the best choice of materials to implement my instructional model?

   Is multimedia more effective than other instructional tools to implement my goals and objectives?

   —Do I need the interactivity provided by multimedia?

   —Do I need the rapid random access of multimedia?

   —Do I need the review capabilities?

   —Do I need a medium that mandates learner input?

   —Do I need a medium with multiple data sources for student exploration and creation?

   Is multimedia more effective than other instructional tools to meet my students' learning needs?

   Could a movie or video offer the same or better examples of events remote in time and space? Are the concepts so abstract that my own lecture would be more productive?

3. If multimedia is the best choice, which multimedia program is needed?

   Is the program to be used as a teaching or learning tool?

   Have I considered the cost? Are the multimedia programs worth the money?

   Will I be able to use the software—are the necessary hardware configurations available or readily accessible?

4. What is the quality of the instructional design?
   Are the examples ethnically and culturally sensitive?
   Are the goals and objectives clear?
   Is the overall organization of the multimedia program clear?
   Are the directions specific?
   Does the program flow in a logical and orderly manner?
   Are directions for help accessible?
   Is appropriate feedback offered?
   Are there opportunities for review when desired?
   Are manuals and other documentation understandable and attractive?
   Can the program be completed in a timely manner?
   Are specific criteria fulfilled?
   If the program is open ended, are there lists of the contents available?
   Are there opportunities for students to learn ways to compile data selected?
   If the program is directive and sequential, do remedial loops offer new material and methodology?
   Are there frequent opportunities for testing?
   Has a management system been set up?
   If the program is group oriented, are there pause points for group discussion?
   Is the content appropriate for group discussion?
5. What is the technical quality of the program?
   Are the color, graphics, and sound supportive of the instructional purpose of the program?
   Are the examples realistic?
   Are the examples relevant and engaging?
   Are the actors and sets authentic?
   Is the text easily read?
   oes the program run reliably?
   Do access mechanisms such as bar code readers and remote control devices function properly?
   Do additional data management tools need to be created?

Example

Building on the information given in previous chapters on defining the problem and generating alternatives, this case illustrates how a professor applies criteria and weighs evidence to make the decision. Although described in a linear fashion, this process is, in fact, interactive.

Selecting an Instructional Model

In a teacher education program in the United States, students were involved in a methods course for social studies. The broad goals for the course (tied to the broad goals of higher education in general) related to cultural diversity in all the complexity of its present and historical dimensions, environmental responsibility, social action, and empowerment. The professor's more specific course goals consisted of students' review and evaluation of currently available materials, and students' creation of new materials for instruction in K-12 social studies classrooms. The course also emphasized use of an inductive, problem solving approach, where an explorative instructional design mode used as a learning tool would be effective.

Students came from predominantly rural and suburban areas with little exposure to cultural diversity. Nonetheless, several American Indian and African-American students were among the thirty enrolled. Results from a "learning styles" inventory administered by the professor indicated that some students felt they learned best primarily through teacher-directed models—clear goals, specific directions, constant guidance in coming up with right answers. Other students preferred more open processes, desiring to create their own theories based on multiple experiences and examples in course concepts and content; some indicated preferences for visual learning while others preferred kinesthetic and auditory modes of learning. Thus, it seemed important to develop a program that allowed flexible use.

Selecting Multimedia as Instructional Tools

To fulfill broad goals for both higher education and course goals and objectives, the professor believed it imperative that the pre-service teachers become familiar with multimedia materials. Because her students were preparing to teach in the twenty-first century, it was crucial that they be knowledgeable about the emerging technologies as both teaching and learning tools. The diversity of student needs in the class also would benefit from the variety of multimedia materials available. In this class, the multimedia applications would be one instructional source among others.

The professor anticipated introducing multimedia programs to the whole class after which small groups of students would explore the programs in a laboratory setting. They would review the materials using carefully designed evaluation criteria. Students could also create software instructional materials for classroom use by using a videodisc, CD-ROM, and Aldus Persuasion with Quick Time in the campus media laboratory. Students would work in small groups to create the materials and then share them with other groups; they would critique their efforts before taking the materials into the elementary schools.

Determining the Instructional Design and Technical Qualities of Multimedia Programs

After the deliberations described above, the professor decided to include multimedia with different formats and levels of quality in instructional design. She reviewed programs available for purchase, such as *GTV: A Geographic Perspective on American History* and *The Powers of the Supreme Court*, using specific criteria. She also reviewed a multimedia program, *Understanding*

Cultural Diversity: A Case Study of Ojibwe Indians, developed at her campus. In applying her criteria, she found GTV allowed both open-ended class presentation and possibilities for sequential interactivity. Individuals or small groups could create their own visual essays through the use of an on-disc program called "Showmaker." The Supreme Court videodisc was a Level One program in its published format. The cultural diversity disc was organized as a Level One database; it included both a videodisc and a CD-ROM disc that could be accessed with a bar code reader.

Further, the professor found that the instructional design for "GTV" centered on the white, Western culture (from 1492 on) although there was a small section on American Indians and a few primary sources from different cultures available. The program was organized logically with clear directions for use. The use of the mouse to access any of the four main parts of the disc made the program user friendly. Any of the material could be reviewed at any time. Because this was not a tutorial, there were no tests or remedial loops. Open-ended editing of disc content was possible. The technical quality of the sound, color, and graphics was exemplary. There were only a few glitches in the sound/visual congruence. The examples were realistic and engaging with authentic recreations of past events.

In applying specific criteria to the "Supreme Court" disc, she found some diversity in the montages included with each provision in the Bill of Rights. The instructional design was quite linear and would need much instructor input to raise discussion questions. The use of a talking head interview format could have been enlivened with more real examples of the court in action. The bar code reader was effective in accessing the information.

In applying the specific criteria to the cultural diversity disc, the professor found that the printed index had some errors in frame numbers that needed correction. It was frustrating when vocabulary words appeared where the index listed a film of life on the reservation.

Determining Hardware Needs

The university had two multimedia Macintosh learning stations in the Media Resources Center. The center was open for twelve hours each day with sign-up sheets for reserving space. The professor demonstrated the discs early in the term to allow time for student groups to review the materials that were on reserve. The hardware was both available and accessible.

A program for compiling the data from the cultural diversity disc would need to be created. The professor would consult expert colleagues and use her own previous work with HyperCard to create a user friendly program for student use.

Making the Choice

After completing the process of applying criteria in the decision making process outlined above, the professor did choose to use all three multimedia programs—*GTV: A Geographic Perspective of American History*, *The Powers of the Supreme Court*, and *Cultural Diversity: A Case Study of Ojibwe Indians*. The first two of these would be used for fulfilling the objective related to critiquing materials, and "GTV" and "Cultural Diversity" would be used to fulfill the objective related to developing new materials. The various designs and concrete examples would allow learning opportunities for both inductive and deductive learners. The examples of cultural diversity (or lack of them) would also be a source of information for discussion. Neither repurposing nor developing an original application was necessary to meet the educational objectives of this course.

Guidelines

In summary, the following are suggested as general guidelines for examining the alternatives and selecting a solution as applied to the use of multimedia in higher education instruction.

1. Determine which instructional model is appropriate to meet the broad goals for higher education, course and lesson objectives, and learner needs.
2. Determine if multimedia is the best teaching/learning tool to use for the teaching/learning model selected.
3. Determine which multimedia format is best for the teaching/learning tool selected and locate or develop programs.
4. Apply criteria to determine the quality of instructional designs for selected multimedia programs.
5. Apply criteria to determine the technical quality of the selected multimedia programs.
6. Analyze the hardware availability for the selected multimedia programs.
7. Choose the program or programs to be used.

Resources

Evaluating Education Software: A Guide for Teachers by Sloane and others (1989) includes consideration of the interdependence of hardware and criteria for evaluating instructional design, program design, management features, and documentation. It also gives suggestions for interpreting formal evaluation data. Checklists for evaluating education software are included.

Littlejohn and Parker (1988) have developed an evaluation methodology for compact discs that includes hardware, software, product content, program management, ease of use, and vendor support. The methodology includes forms for CD-ROM student evaluation as well as product evaluation.

Professional conferences represent another possible source of information. For example, the Society for Application of Learning Technologies (SALT) offers preconference workshops, sessions, and displays that highlight how to evaluate instructional technology. Organizations in specific disciplines frequently have Special Interest Group (SIG) demonstration laboratories and papers about multimedia. For example, the National Council for the Social Studies has a computer/media laboratory where faculty can review current hardware configurations as well as software with both video and text (CD-I) options. Faculty can also learn ways to evaluate multimedia programs for inclusion in courses.

Journals, either those related directly to technology, such as those listed in the appendix or those pertaining to a specific content area, can be consulted. Most academic fields now have journals that review software for that discipline. For example, *The History Microcomputer Review* carries critical reviews of currently available software for that area of study. Reviews in specific disciplines address the choices that must be made in including multimedia in instruction.

Conclusion

In evaluating the design and technical quality of computer-based instructional programs, you must apply new criteria that are emerging for multimedia products. These criteria include consideration of the effects of the masses of materials available through the programs on the learners' creation of their own "visual essays."

The process of selecting an appropriate multimedia program involves several steps. It is important that you identify the instructional model that fulfills the identified goals and objectives. It is necessary that you determine which format, which group configuration (individual, small group, large group), and which tool (teaching or learning) will be needed. You must locate appropriate, cost-effective multimedia programs and, through the application of general and specific criteria, determine the quality of the instructional design and the technical quality of those programs. As you examine various products, you should investigate the availability and accessibility of hardware needed to use them. After addressing these issues, you can decide which multimedia program or programs to use.

CHAPTER 10

IMPLEMENTING THE SOLUTION: USING MULTIMEDIA AS A TEACHING AND LEARNING TOOL

Goals

Multimedia offers significant advantages over other teaching and learning activities, but to be effective it must be used properly. A key aspect of multimedia instruction is *interactivity*; therefore, it is important to understand this concept and how it can be used with multimedia. When a particular multimedia program has been selected for a specific teaching or learning experience, the instructor must locate all necessary hardware and rehearse or practice with the particular program. This chapter delineates the nature of interactivity and highlights steps in using multimedia.

General Information

Needs Peculiar to Multimedia

Unlike a lecture that can be written (typed, word processed) and then delivered with relatively little physical preparation, new multimedia programs are often more complex. Because no common standards yet exist across all software programs and hardware configurations, set-up can be confusing to the novice. See Chapter 4 for a review of the hardware available.

Interactivity — A Review of the Literature

Conceptions of learning range from viewing the learner as a passive recipient of stimuli to seeing the learner as an active constructor of meaning. Each of these views suggests a different type of interactivity. Jonassen (1985) defines levels of interactivity arranged from specific to general, according to a learner's actions in relationship to the instructional technology. Consideration of the design's level of intelligence, the type of interactive program, the level of processing, the modalities used, and the tasks (content and process) to be completed are important in determining the type of interactivity desired.

Beyond the mere action of pressing a key or of manipulating a mouse, Carlson and Falk (1990) have outlined two main types of interactive models available in multimedia. One is an instructional system that gives correct information, tests, and remedials; here, the learner's interactivity involves regurgitating information given and responding to test items. The second is an instructional system in which the learner chooses what to learn and/or chooses how to learn the material; here, the instructional system acts interactively by providing content options and/or learning options.

Lucas (1992) echoes these models by describing an instructional technology in which the learner uses simple physical or cognitive manipulations to react to instruction (*reactive* model). She further describes instructional activities in which learners construct and deduce principles from their actions and experiences in a *proactive* manner. A third model, *interactive*, describes an environment in which the learner branches through a program based on responses to questions posed by the computer. Lucas maintains that each of the models has a specific purpose. The reactive model is useful in polishing a basic skill, the interactive model is appropriate for a novice learner of knowledge, and the proactive model is successfully used by those with some experience and knowledge in the subject.

Multimedia, with its nonlinear, nonsequential arrangements of material, and with its large capacity for storage of print, video, and stills, offers opportunities for the interactive and proactive learning models. Whether the multimedia is used in a video-enhanced didactic lecture or in exploration by individual learners, it is important to involve the learners in creating new levels of understanding and more encompassing cognitive structures through which to process new information. Assuring that interactive models of teaching and learning are, in fact, used with the multimedia programs also requires special attention. Instructors sometimes become so easily lost in the technicalities of cable connection and audio clarity that they neglect the instructional tasks of involving the learner.

Steps in Locating and Setting Up Hardware

In addition to having considerations of interactivity, instructors must engage in the logistics of locating and setting up the hardware for a specific learning experience. The instructor must first find out what hardware is needed and then how to obtain and set up that equipment.

For a Level One application, the common equipment is a videodisc and/or a CD-ROM player, a monitor (or television set), a bar code reader or a remote control device, and, sometimes, an overhead projector adapted for use with computer screens. These components need to be connected with suitable cables.

For a Level Three multimedia application, the common equipment is a videodisc and/or CD-ROM player, a monitor, and a computer. Again, if the application is to be used in a group, some type of amplification of the computer screen is usually necessary.

Steps in Rehearsing with the Multimedia Program

Once the hardware has been set up, the professor will likely have the best results if he or she takes the time to rehearse the selected application. The appropriate interactivity—reactive, proactive, and interactive—must be identified as a guide to the rehearsal. Chapter 5 describes five instructional models with different types of interactivity—video enhanced presentation, exploration, structured observation, simulation, and assessment and focused instruction. Whereas video-enhanced presentations are primarily teaching tools with which the teacher directs instruction (interactive), assessment and focused instruction is usually a tool with which a learner works with an individualized multimedia learning station following a carefully designed computer program (reactive). The other models—exploration, structured observation, and simulation—can be used effectively in either teacher or learner formats. For example, a teacher could use a multimedia program in an open-ended (exploratory, simulation, structured observation) manner as part of a discussion or presentation with either a large or small group. A learner could also use these types of multimedia programs similarly at a learning station in a laboratory. The steps described here illustrate different approaches based on different combinations of instructional models as they are used in teaching and learning.

Learning station use. If students are to use the software in an individual learning station in a laboratory setting, the professor should first determine that enough machines exist for the students to use them within a reasonable period of time. The instructor should "walk through" the program first and determine whether directions exist for equipment use—from turning the system on to loading the software. Then, the professor should determine how to save student responses that may be needed for evaluation purposes. In using the program, glitches can be noted and communicated to students. Students are particularly frustrated when they cannot exit a program. The manuals and other documentation that accompany the software should be easy to use with clear directions. Use of laboratory assistants helps students gain confidence in using the new multimedia.

If a small group uses the learning station format in a laboratory setting, the professor also needs to review the material for the technical aspects noted above. In addition, he or she should provide structure and support for the group experience. For example, if the program will be used as an exploratory model (proactive interactivity) from which examples will be chosen and a "new" visual essay created, then the instructor must test the cut-and-paste directions. If using a simulation program in which situations must be discussed before group entries are made, then stop-and-discuss pause points need clarification. Instruction is more effective by scheduling frequent, but shorter laboratory periods.

Class use. If intending to use the multimedia program to complement class lectures, the instructor should rehearse the lecture along with the visual/auditory additions from the multimedia in a way that maximizes interactivity. For example, if several branches are available, a walkthrough demonstration of how to make a choice and enter it into the program would be needed. The students must be shown how to navigate a multimedia resource in different ways and how to use the flexibility of programs.

The rehearsal should take place at the site in which the lecture is to be given. This is to ensure that all projections are clear, that images are visible from various parts of the room(s), and that all cables and hardware components are in working order. Of particular importance is the bar code reader—are there particular ways that the reader must be held and moved in order for program access to occur smoothly? It is important to have a back-up remote control to use if the bar code reader does not work.

On the other hand, if the structured observation model is used, then the professor needs to be sure that the program functions well, allowing appropriate stop points for interactions among students before the media program continues. A clear plan of how the interactions among students and professor will occur help ensure maximum interactivity.

Sometimes it may be necessary that the instructor develops a multimedia learning station by collecting the appropriate hardware and putting all the elements together. Here, observation of various hardware configurations by colleagues in other settings should be helpful. Collecting the needed cables to connect a videodisc, CD-ROM drive, printer, videotape player, scanner, and other components can be complex. Arrangement of such hardware also can be cumbersome, whether in classroom or laboratory.

Questions

In implementing a multimedia program in a particular instructional setting, the following questions can be asked:

1. How will I guide the desired interactivity—reactive, interactive, proactive?
    How will I ensure that these type(s) of interactivity happen?
2. How can the appropriate hardware be located and set up?
    What are the hardware requirements for the multimedia program?
    What resources and expertise are available on campus?
    — Through the software company?
    — Through local hardware companies?
    — Through networks on e-mail?
3. What steps are needed for effective rehearsal using multimedia programs?
    In a laboratory setting,
    — Is the equipment ready to use?
    — Are the directions clear?
    — Is the documentation easily understood?
    — Have management systems been set up?

— Have any glitches been identified and ways to deal with them described?

— Is a laboratory assistant available?

— If necessary, is a user-friendly program for creating "visual essays" available and easily used?

In a class setting,

— Is the equipment ready to use?

— Can the visual sequences be seen from all parts of the room?

— Do bar code readers or remote control devices work properly?

— Has the professor identified the exact examples to be used?

— Has the professor identified and practiced the strategies that allow interactivity to occur?

Examples

Example from a Class Setting

The professor had developed a lecture about the effects of air pollution on the environment. He wished to have an interactive lecture with concrete examples for analysis. In the campus media center, he reviewed various multimedia programs for visual images to enhance and illustrate the lecture. A colleague from the media center assisted in the organization of the examples using a bar code creation program. After the examples were organized in the lab, the professor reserved the portable multimedia hardware module for the classroom. He then went through a dress rehearsal, connecting the cable, adjusting the LCD overhead and the monitor screens for maximum visibility throughout the room.

The professor showed before/after pollution scenes. He wanted to be sure that he could move back and forth between the scenes and allow multiple observations of events. In several instances, the visual examples formed a set of data from which the students could draw conclusions about the effects of pollution. By raising questions, setting expectations, and offering multiple examples, the professor hoped to encourage students' observations and making generalizations from data. This type of interactivity would increase understanding and cognitive strategizing. Because all aspects of the presentation had been rehearsed, the program facilitated interactivity, allowing students to take the initiative.

Example Using a Learning Center Setting

Each student in a liberal education environmental education class had been asked to prepare a visual essay from the *Visual Almanac* disc showing the effects of pollution in various parts of the world. Before sending the students to the learning laboratory, the professor demonstrated the equipment, creating a short visual essay as the students observed.

The professor set up learning stations in the student cooperative learning laboratory. Each of the learning stations had a Macintosh computer with a videodisc player and a CD-ROM drive with encyclopedic information. The *Visual Almanac* disc was in the player and equipment was ready to be used. A special, user-friendly HyperCard program to compile the data selected had been developed by a colleague. Before they came to the laboratory class, students had reviewed the *Visual Almanac* annotated index, which was available for reference as the students worked. The students were able to begin their selection of examples and to write the word-processed text to accompany each of the selections. Later, these essays would be presented to the class.

Example Using an Individualized Tutorial Program

A professor of mathematics was teaching a beginning course in statistical concepts. She was concerned because some of the students did not have the prerequisite knowledge in areas such as nominal and ordinal levels of measurement. After selecting a videodisc tutorial program entitled *Descriptive Statistics*, she used the campus learning laboratory to "test" it.

She reviewed the documentation that described how to load the program and how to access the help screens that were available. The directions were clear and usable. As she progressed through the instructional program, she reviewed the tests and found them to be acceptable. The remedial loops appeared to function properly.

Because she wanted a printout of student progress, she asked the laboratory assistant to set up the monitoring system. Each time one of her students used the laboratory, the professor received a student progress record. The laboratory monitor would always be available to provide needed help to the students.

The next day the professor announced this support option to the class. The tutorial would be effective in meeting the needs of individual students in this large section.

Guidelines

In summary, guidelines for implementing a specific multimedia program include the following:

1. Decide on the appropriate type of interactivity—proactive, interactive, or reactive.
2. Set up appropriate hardware by using expertise and resources from
   — on-campus personnel
   — hardware company personnel
   — software program personnel
   — experts contacted through e-mail networks.
3. Rehearse the multimedia application.
   a. For laboratory learning station approaches, be sure the equipment works properly, that directions are clear, and that assistance is available.
   b. For in-class use, walk through the program *in the classroom* to ensure smooth functioning and optimum viewing.

    c. Check to ensure that the type of interactivity chosen is, in fact, possible through the configurations of hardware and software that are used.

4. Use the rehearsed program for instruction in the course.

Resources

Many resources exist that describe active learning and the roles of the learner. Those that apply specifically to multimedia have been cited in the text. For a more complete review of the ideas, please consult the following sources. Page (1990) has clarified the concept of active learning and discussed the use and value of active learning models. Bonwell and Eison (1991) have described the nature of active learning at the higher education as well as specific ways that faculty can implement active learning techniques.

Fortunately, a college professor usually has a variety of places to go for assistance. On campus, staff in the computer or media center often have expertise in setting up hardware configurations. Colleagues with special skills are often pleased to help. Observing colleagues using multimedia applications in class can also suggest various ways to use multimedia programs with different types of interactivity.

Local computer companies have educational representatives who can assist with hardware questions. Documentation manuals available with software programs usually have specific instructions for the hardware requirements as well as telephone help numbers for personalized assistance.

More broadly, being enrolled in a national or international e-mail network can be productive. Experts from various areas can answer questions raised about hardware.

Conclusion

After the professor has selected instructional models and specific software programs for class use, he or she must rehearse its presentation. Steps in the rehearsal process vary depending on whether an individualized learning station or a classroom application is used. It is important to rehearse the application in the actual setting. The realization of the full benefits of multimedia instruction requires genuine interactivity in which learners are engaged cognitively and emotionally.

CHAPTER 11

EVALUATING THE USE OF MULTIMEDIA

Goals

An important part of any instruction, from both a problem solving and instructional design point of view, is the evaluation phase. While it is usually considered at the end of an instructional development process, the evaluation phase actually encompasses the entire project, aimed from beginning to end at improving the quality of the instruction. It is important, therefore, to understand how both formative evaluation, i.e., efforts to improve the multimedia instruction; and summative evaluation, i.e., efforts to assess the worth of the multimedia instruction, can be undertaken effectively.

General Information

Formative Evaluation

During the developmental process, formative evaluation helps the developer of a multimedia application increase the likelihood that the final product will achieve its stated goals (Flagg, 1990). Flagg defines four phases of formative evaluation for educational technologies: (1) needs assessment occurs during the planning phase of program development, (2) pre-production formative evaluation takes place during the design phase, (3) production formative evaluation occurs during the production phase, and (4) implementation formative evaluation occurs when the application is actually in use.

Needs assessment formative evaluation emphasizes the significance of developing goals appropriate to the learning setting. In general, sound instructional design dictates that the goals of instruction should be derived from learning needs. These needs can be identified from pre-testing or from interviews or questionnaires of either students or teachers. Reeves (1989) also stresses the importance of assessing the worth of the project objectives in the context of the institutional needs.

Pre-production and production formative evaluation focus on providing the most effective multimedia program for the goals identified. Several continuing issues can be addressed, such as how to improve the instructional product, the delivery system, and the instructional design system (Reeves, 1989).

123

Instructional design reviews during the process of developing your own applications or repurposing applications can consist of asking colleagues or students to evaluate preliminary flowcharts or storyboards. After production of video or audio, reviews of all possible video and audio can assist in determining which material will actually be included in the final application. Chapter 9 provides a variety of criteria to consider during this type of evaluation.

Implementation formative evaluation, also termed "beta testing," involves having learners actually use the application and the equipment, and obtaining information on their effectiveness as an instructional tool. Chapters 9 and 10 provide numerous questions that can guide this type of formative evaluation. One-to-one and small group use of the application can be useful (Dick & Carey, 1990), and direct observation, interviews, questionnaires, paper-based tests, multimedia-based tests, and tracking of learner choices are all methods of obtaining information that can provide guidance in improving the multimedia application's overall effectiveness (Savenye, 1992).

Summative Evaluation

Summative evaluation focuses on assessing the worth of a multimedia application. Attention to immediate effectiveness evaluation, impact evaluation, and/or cost-effectiveness evaluation can guide summative evaluations (Reeves, 1989). Immediate effectiveness evaluation focuses on determining whether instructional goals have been achieved, whether learners were satisfied with the instruction, and whether learning was efficient (less time for a particular level of goal achievement). Impact evaluation attempts to determine whether learning was transferred from the multimedia learning setting to the setting in which knowledge and skills are to be used. Cost-effectiveness evaluation seeks to determine the delivery costs for multimedia instruction, sometimes in comparison to other forms of instruction.

Numerous summative evaluation studies of multimedia applications, mostly videodisc-based, have been reported. Reviews of these studies indicate a variety of positive outcomes in terms of immediate effectiveness. Drake (1987) summarized the major findings of existing research and concluded that, in a variety of applications, compared with "traditional instruction," interactive videodisc instruction led to greater learner satisfaction, reduced instruction time, and equivalent or improved effectiveness. Reeves (1989) reports that interactive video can offer advantages over other types of instruction in terms of cost, safety, flexibility, efficiency, and effectiveness. Bosco (1986), DeBloois (1988), and Slee (1990) also found that instruction incorporating interactive videodiscs generally helped students learn better than traditional instruction. Bosco (1986) and Savenye (1990) cautioned, however, that studies using statistical analysis tended to lessen differences between instructional methods.

McNeil and Nelson (1991) conducted a meta-analysis of studies that evaluated the cognitive achievement of learners who used interactive videodisc instruction. They analyzed sixty-three studies that incorporated learning measures and an experimental or quasi-experimental design. Their analysis indicated that interactive video is effective for instruction and was somewhat more effective when used in groups rather than individually.

Proposed Evaluation Focus

After reviewing existing studies on multimedia and the results of their own studies, Falk and Carlson (1991) identified three main factors that impacted the outcomes of multimedia instruction: (1) the characteristics of the learners, (2) the instructional models used within the multimedia application, and (3) the manner in which the application was used, with learning processes being a mediating factor. These issues are graphically represented in Figure 11-1.

Future evaluation research, both formative and summative in nature, must address these key issues. Formative evaluation should continue systematically to seek information that will improve multimedia applications and their use with various types of learners, incorporating the four separate types of formative evaluation conceptualized by Flagg (1990). Needs assessment formative evaluation should more precisely define the relevant learner styles and characteristics. Preproduction and production formative evaluation can focus on conceptualizing and improving the instructional models most appropriately suited to multimedia instruction and to the specific learner characteristics that are present. Implementation formative evaluation can examine and define the ways in which multimedia applications can be most effectively used. The goal of these formative evaluation studies is to build upon the advantages of multimedia, such as

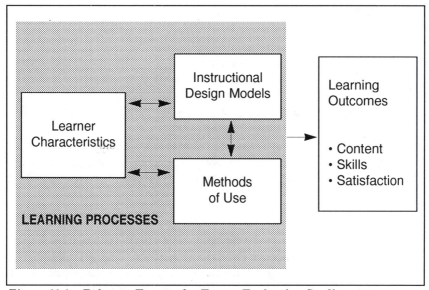

Figure 11.1   **Relevant Factors for Future Evaluation Studies**

interactivity, visual capabilities, and individualization, and to design and use each multimedia application in such a way as to maximize positive outcomes for specific learners.

Future summative evaluation studies should focus on whether, and why, multimedia applications are superior to other forms of instruction in achieving certain kinds of learning outcomes. The results reported below suggest that the effectiveness of designs and uses of multimedia applications varies; some multimedia applications are superior on certain criteria to the instruction previously used in human service and teacher education. Future summative evaluation studies should examine the cost effectiveness of various uses of applications incorporating different instructional models in achieving positive results among learners with different characteristics. These studies should also focus on the learning processes that occur with particular combinations of learners, instructional designs, and uses.

New types of research and evaluation must be undertaken to accomplish the formative and summative tasks identified above. Multivariate analysis can assist researchers in examining the variety of factors that may affect the outcomes achieved in using a particular application in a specific way with various learners. Marlino (1990) advocates a causal modeling approach that can simultaneously examine relationships among a number of factors, such as those identified above. Future evaluation should also put greater emphasis on front-end conceptualization of studies that adopt a prescriptive, as opposed to descriptive, methodology (Clark, 1989).

Questions

1. How can multimedia instruction be improved?
   — While defining the problem?
   — While generating the multimedia solutions?
   — While implementing the solution?
2. Is multimedia instruction meeting the instructional goals?
   — In terms of acquisition of knowledge and skills?
   — In terms of satisfaction with instruction?
   — In terms of efficiency of instruction?
3. What is the impact and cost effectiveness of the multimedia instruction?
4. What methods of use and models of instruction are effective in achieving specific types of educational goals for learners with particular characteristics?

Examples

Multimedia applications have been used in over thirty classes in the College of Education and Human Service Professions over the past six years. Samples of the various formative and summative evaluation studies provide examples of the types of evaluation activities that can occur in higher education.

Formative Evaluation

Approximately fifteen of the evaluation studies conducted in CEHSP have been formative in nature. While all four types of formative evaluation identified by Flagg (1990) have been used in the college, the studies reported below will focus on implementation formative evaluations that have been conducted after the applications had been initially completed and before they had taken final form.

A series of formative evaluation studies were conducted on the *Understanding Groups* videodisc application. An initial evaluation involved systematically observing several undergraduate teacher education students in using the application as a learning tool. The results indicated that one phase of instruction, the inductive track, took too long to complete, that students needed more orientation and instructions for certain segments of instruction, and that students' attention and enthusiasm diminished after about one hour of instruction. Consequently, the inductive track was shortened, clearer instructions were incorporated into computer text, and the length of time that the application was used in one session was limited.

Portions of the *Understanding Groups* application were used as a teaching tool in two separate graduate social work courses on human behavior. The instructor introduced concepts related to shared leadership and then used the application to show video segments of group behavior. The evaluation form used in this study, and in all subsequent formative studies reported in this section, asked students to provide (1) a global rating of the value of the instruction on a seven-point scale, (2) advantages of the instruction, (3) disadvantages of the instruction, and (4) suggestions for improving the portion of the class that used videodisc applications. The results showed the instruction to be rated as very valuable in one class and only of average value in the other, despite very similar instruction being provided. The advantages identified included the visual and auditory learning opportunities, real life examples, and seeing how different group behaviors led to different outcomes in an application section of the instruction. Disadvantages included difficulty in reading the text on the projection system and the fast pace of the instruction.

Two other formative evaluation studies have examined the use of the *Southeast Asian Refugee* application as a teaching tool in courses on human diversity. Taken primarily by sophomores majoring in teacher education or a related human service profession, students in both studies reported the application to be quite valuable. They cited seeing and hearing realistic experiences, the variety of information available, and the efficiency of being selective in viewing as advantages. Several students mentioned the quick pace of instruction as a disadvantage, but two others reported the instruction to be too slow. The most common suggestion was more use of videodisc instruction in the future.

A series of three formative evaluation studies were conducted on the repurposed *Psychology Encyclopedia* application. The program was used in separate offerings of a human development course taken primarily by sophomores in teaching or other human service education majors. These uses were again rated as very valuable, averaging over 6.2 on a seven-point scale. The clear visual images in general and the ability to go instantly from one still to another to compare various stages of prenatal development were frequently cited as advantages. While few students identified disadvantages, those who did mentioned that the screen size of the monitor was too small in the larger class and that the pictures sometimes distracted the students from what was being said. Suggestions for improvement included various ideas for making the video images easier to see. Students again expressed an interest in using more videodiscs for instruction in the future.

Summative Evaluation

Four summative evaluative research studies have attempted to determine if the different uses of videodisc applications lead to positive learning outcomes. The positive outcomes that served as dependent measures in these studies always included acquisition of knowledge, satisfaction with the instruction, and perceived value of the instruction as obtained by students using paper and pencil measures. Other dependent measures are described with the results of the individual studies.

The first study compared the use of two different tracks of videodisc instruction to a traditional classroom approach in teaching about group dynamics (Carlson and Falk, 1989). Junior and senior elementary teacher education students were randomly assigned to three instructional groups to learn about shared leadership and cooperative goals and learning: videodisc inductive track, videodisc deductive track, and a reading/lecture/discussion activity that had previously been used to teach this same material.

The results indicated the students using the videodisc instruction as a learning tool (whether the inductive or deductive track) obtained significantly higher scores on the test on content acquisition than did those students participating in the reading/lecture/discussion group. Students in the videodisc inductive group received significantly higher scores on a test of group observation skills than did students in either of the other groups. In terms of impact evaluation, students in the videodisc inductive group had higher group facilitation scores when observed actually working with elementary students in cooperative learning groups than did those in the videodisc deductive group. The videodisc deductive students took far less time to complete the instruction than did the other two groups. There were no differences among the three groups on measures of overall satisfaction with the instruction. The groups did report using different thinking skills in completing the instruction, with students in the videodisc inductive group engaging in higher-level thinking skills, such as synthesizing and evaluating, than students in the other groups.

A second study compared two different models of videodisc applications to a traditional classroom approach of teaching about human diversity (Falk, 1989).

Undergraduate human service and teacher education students taking a required course in human diversity were randomly assigned to one of three groups: (1) students using the videodisc on *Southeast Asian Refugees* individually as a learning tool, (2) an instructor using the *Southeast Asian Refugees* videodisc as a teaching tool to instruct students in the classroom, and (3) an instructor showing a videotape and leading a discussion in the traditional method of covering the material on Southeast Asian Refugees in the course.

The results indicated that both of the groups using videodisc instruction scored significantly higher on a test of content acquisition than did the group using the traditional videotape and discussion instruction. The traditional instruction and the videodisc instruction completed in the classroom by the instructor were both rated as significantly more valuable than the instruction using the videodisc as a learning tool.

A third study compared two different tracks of videodisc instruction to outside reading as a method of learning about group dynamics. Six different groups were formed by randomly assigning junior and senior students in an elementary teaching methods course to work alone or in pairs using either (1) videodisc inductive instruction, (2) videodisc deductive instruction, or (3) a specified set of reading materials to learn shared leadership and group goals.

The results indicated that both the videodisc inductive groups, whether working alone or in pairs, and the videodisc deductive groups working in pairs, scored significantly higher on content and observation skill acquisition than did the reading groups. Students in both of the videodisc deductive groups reported greater satisfaction with the instruction and used significantly less time to complete the instruction than did the other four groups. The videodisc groups were significantly more satisfied on several dimensions of the instruction, including receiving useful and appropriate feedback, helpful summaries, and a variety of response modes.

A fourth study also compared the effectiveness of different methods of using videodisc applications in an elementary education teaching methods course (Carlson, 1991). Students were randomly assigned to four instructional groups using the *Understanding Groups* videodisc application: (1) peer-taught small group using an inductive design of instruction, (2) peer-taught small group using a deductive design of instruction, (3) individualized learning using an inductive design of instruction, and (4) individualized learning using a deductive design of instruction. As in the above studies, students were to learn basic concepts about group interaction and how to observe various group behaviors.

Results were obtained by using a multivariate analysis of variance with three independent variables (small groups or individualized format, inductive or deductive design of instruction, and match or nonmatch of learning style to design of instruction) and four dependent variables (content scores, observation skill scores, overall satisfaction, and attitude toward learner control of instruction). Content scores were not significantly different. Observation skill scores were significantly higher if learner style (deductive or inductive) was matched to the design of the instruction. Overall satisfaction was significantly greater for students in small groups. Students in the individualized format agreed more strongly that they controlled the pace and sequence of instruction.

Guidelines

1. Engage in formative evaluation throughout the process of addressing an educational problem with multimedia.
2. Thorough definition of the problem (see Chapter 3), careful examination of the possible multimedia solutions along a variety of dimensions (see Chapter 9), and purposeful preparation for implementation (see Chapter 10) are sound investments in improving the success of using a multimedia application.
3. Systematically assess the degree to which educational goals have been achieved, focusing on acquisition of knowledge and skills, student satisfaction with the multimedia instruction, efficiency of the instruction, and other goals relevant to your educational problem.
4. Recognize that learner characteristics, methods of using multimedia, and models of instruction may all interact to determine the effectiveness of achieving different types of educational goals. If possible, build consideration of these factors into summative evaluations.
5. Consider impact effectiveness and cost effectiveness of multimedia applications whenever possible.

Resources

A number of resources are available to guide the effective evaluation of multimedia instruction. Flagg (1990) provides helpful guidelines and specific examples of the kinds of formative evaluation that can improve multimedia development and use. Other books that include at least an informative chapter on evaluation appropriate for interactive technologies include Dick and Carey (1990) and Johnson and Foa (1989).

Periodicals and conference proceedings regularly include articles describing guidelines and methods for conducting multimedia evaluations or examples of how multimedia instruction has been evaluated. Examples of journals having a higher proportion of evaluation related articles include *Educational Technology* and *Educational Technology Research and Development*. Specific articles on evaluation of multimedia include one by Reeves (1986), which addresses models for research and evaluation of interactive video; by Savenye (1992), on alternative methods for conducting formative evaluations of interactive instruction; by Falk and Carlson (1991), on evaluating multimedia; and by Clark (1989), on future directions for research in instructional technology.

Conferences of interest include preconference tutorials or sessions that focus on the evaluation of multimedia. The SALT (Society for the Application of Learning

Technologies) conferences in Orlando in February and in Washington (D.C.) in August are examples of meetings that cover evaluation of instructional methods.

Conclusion

It is important to evaluate multimedia instruction at least partly because the technique is so new that most instructors lack experience in what is or is not effective. Formative evaluation assists faculty members in providing the best possible multimedia instruction; summative evaluation determines whether multimedia instruction is effective in terms of achieving the identified educational goals. By focusing on what type of multimedia instruction most closely achieves specific kinds of educational goals for students with particular characteristics, its appropriate role can be more clearly identified.

PART 4

The Future and Conclusion

Parts 1, 2, and 3 provide basic information on what you currently need to know to develop and use multimedia in higher education. Part 4 examines the future of multimedia, revisits some key points, and concludes with thoughts on the role of multimedia in higher education.

Chapter 12 examines the possible, probable, and preferable futures related to multimedia. The trends in higher education and multimedia hardware and its applications are described, and the possible implications of developments in related technologies explored. Scenarios describe education involving multimedia in the future. Whether in the case studies provided or related to multimedia more generally, the nature of the future use of multimedia is being created today.

Chapter 13 provides a brief review of the problem solving process and describes some of the steps to get started in using multimedia. The chapter concludes by examining the niche for multimedia in higher education, both in the current setting and as higher education and multimedia may develop in the future.

CHAPTER 12

THE FUTURE OF MULTIMEDIA

Goals

Because multimedia hardware and software, and issues in higher education in general, change so rapidly, it is important to anticipate what the future may hold. This chapter explores what is possible, probable, and preferable for multimedia in higher education and examines what educators can do to create for multimedia in higher education a future that combines the best of technology and instructional methods.

General Information

The Futurist Perspective

Persons interested in a particular discipline develop a way of thinking about the topics most relevant to their studies. Those interested in the choices about what we make and buy, for example, have developed a particular perspective; they use concepts such as supply and demand and gross domestic product to understand the dynamics of economic systems. A psychological perspective informs people about individual human behavior, and a physics perspective provides insight into physical relationships. In the same way, those interested in the coming events have developed a futurist perspective (Falk, 1980).

The futurist perspective relies on a number of concepts that help organize one's thoughts about next year, the next decade, or the next century. A basic premise is the *non-existence of the future*, which emphasizes that the past and present have some basis in concrete reality, but the future does not. All that we have to indicate what may happen are *images of the future*, that is, mental concepts about what the future may hold.

Futurists also believe in the concept of *alternative* futures, and many believe that the future should be considered in terms of possible, probable, and preferable images (Amara, 1981). *Possible futures* refer to the myriad options of what may occur; *probable futures* are the most likely of the possibilities, based on trends and other factors influencing what the future will bring; *preferable futures* are value laden because they refer to the possibilities that most of us would most like to see come about.

The futurist perspective also incorporates a systems approach, a long-term time frame, and characteristic methodologies. The *systems approach* emphasizes the interconnected nature of the world in which all actions affect one another. The *long-term time frame* suggests that one must look further into the future— one to twenty years—based in part on an understanding of the past. *Futurist methodologies* include trend extrapolation, computer simulations, relevance trees, and scenarios or stories about the future.

A final key concept is the idea of *creating the future*. If the future does not exist but we are influenced by its images, then both the deliberate actions and lack of actions of today will create the world in which we live tomorrow. More specifically, if we identify the probable future, we can anticipate forces that may be beneficial to us and use them to our advantage in reaching our goals. In imaging what we would like to happen, we can work toward achieving a preferable future.

The Future of Higher Education

A number of possibilities exist for higher education, many of which were touched upon in Chapter 3. The images of probable futures that emerge from among the possibilities, however, seem more relevant. If higher education will likely be increasingly called upon for greater accountability among a group of students of greater diversity, multimedia educational systems must be designed to take these factors into account. If students' learning styles are increasingly visually oriented, for example, then multimedia applications should emphasize full-motion video and still pictures.

The images of preferable futures for higher education are also significant. If we see the greater use and integration of multimedia in higher education as a preferable image, we must clarify that image and begin to work toward bringing it to reality. If we see an increase in individualized education as a desired development, then emphasizing the use of multimedia as a learning tool would help to incorporate that image into a preferred future.

The Future of Multimedia Hardware and Applications

Multimedia hardware continues to develop rapidly, and the future promises that almost anything is possible. Computers continue to become faster, smaller, more powerful, and less expensive. Hard drives provide more storage and less cost per unit. On the other hand, videodisc players and CD-ROM drives have been relatively more stable, trending toward combining features and adding a few bells and whistles, with prices steady or slightly reduced.

Almost all trends point to an increasing emphasis on a digital environment for multimedia (Galbreath, 1992a, 1992b). New hardware such as DVI (digital video interactive) and software such as QuickTime are making digital video much more available, and almost every other capability of multimedia now can be digitized efficiently. While videodiscs are still the most cost-efficient method to provide high-quality video, the probable future is digital.

The number and variety of multimedia applications continues to increase, and steady growth characterizes the market for videodisc applications. The *Videodisc Compendium*, when first published in 1988, listed 400 laserdisc titles; just six years later, the 1994 edition includes over 2,800 titles from more than 250 producers. Whether this growth will be sustained with the increasing emphasis on digital hardware is difficult to forecast.

The numbers of digitally-based applications have increased even more rapidly. *CD-ROMs in Print* listed a few hundred titles when it was first published a few years ago; it now lists over 3,500 titles. The number of applications currently being developed with DVI and QuickTime nearly assures the continued growth of digital applications.

Multimedia and Related Technologies

A number of related technologies are developing such that their futures may intersect with multimedia. These technologies and their possible relation to multimedia are described below.

Distance education. A set of technologies has come to be associated with distance education, in which the instructor or instructional materials and the students may be physically separate from one another. One model of distance education emphasizes sending an educational program from one site to students in other sites around the state, country, or world. A second model involves interactive classrooms in which the teacher, a camera, and a TV screen are in one location and one or more groups of students also have a camera and TV screen in a location remote from the instructor. These educational programs are typically transmitted via satellite or fiber optics, and are often referred to as interactive TV (ITV).

In the future, multimedia may merge with distance education. If one uses the first model described above, the future may see a multimedia application in one location that can be accessed by students hundreds or thousands of miles away via fiber optics or satellite. And if one uses the second model, an instructor could use a multimedia application as a teaching tool in one location and students could experience the application in other remote locations. Each multimedia platform would include a camera on top of the monitor screen so that an individual instructor could be viewed in the digital video box of the screen at any other location. The instructor could thus home in on one student or see a composite collection of individual students that could change as the instructor chose. The student could focus entirely on the multimedia application, see the instructor in the digital box, or check in on other students, again according to the student's choice.

Virtual reality. Computer-generated environments that simulate reality and allow for realistic methods of inputting actions that affect the simulated environment have come to be known as *virtual reality*. Helsel (1992) suggests that the term as currently used describes a gamut of technologies, including artificial reality and cyberspace. Spring (1991) proposes virtual reality hardware and software that provide a sense of (1) inclusion or immersion, (2) navigation, and (3) manipulation. Spring further describes three variables in virtual reality: (1) user's level of control, (2) nature of the reality base, and (3) naturalness of the interaction.

Virtual reality and multimedia may merge in the future, making the dimensions described above even more relevant. Helsel (1992) forecasts two major changes in the educative process stimulated by virtual reality. First, learning via printed images in textbooks will shift to learning via simulations. For example, rather than reading about an historical event, students will be able to experience the event as a simulation and interact with simulated persons from that historical era.   Second, virtual reality provides the potential to move education from reliance on the written text to reliance on symbols and imagery. Because people grasp images more quickly than they can understand numbers or lines of text, use of symbols and imagery may lead to significantly more efficient learning. Much of what will be possible with virtual reality will also be possible with multimedia, particularly as they merge in the future.

Integrated learning systems. Integrated learning systems (ILSs) are networked computers providing individualized instruction and assessment to achieve specified objectives in the context of a standard curriculum, used now more often in elementary and secondary schools (Bailey, 1992). These systems, according to Bailey (ibid., p. 4), can "randomly generate problems, adjust the difficulty and sequence of problems based on student performance, and provide appropriate and immediate feedback (in private)."

In the future, aspects of ILSs may merge with multimedia for use in higher education settings. This image of the future suggests that multimedia applications may be physically housed in digital form in a host computer with connections to individual terminals throughout a campus, a community, or the world (see "distance education" section above). Students at remote terminals may select learning objectives, be provided with individualized multimedia instruction related to those objectives, and be assessed on how well they grasp the relevant concepts. Instructors could monitor student performance via the record keeping capabilities of the ILSs and provide remedial, developmental, or enrichment activities to the individual students as appropriate.

Probable futures for multimedia and other technologies. While it is difficult to forecast the mutual effect of rapidly changing technologies, current trends suggest that multimedia will be influenced by the other technologies described above. As applications become increasingly digitized and compressed, they likely will be transmitted to remote sites. Some aspects of virtual reality will likely enter multimedia applications, and computers will likely be networked and able to share applications.

Models and Methods of Future Use

New models of instruction and methods for using multimedia are emerging. Some examples of these possible futures are described below.

Possible new models of instruction. Dede (1992) suggests that multimedia has the potential to promote metacognition (thinking about thinking) in students. He says that multimedia can provide virtual worlds that students could not otherwise enter—they can also interact in these worlds. Dede proposes that multimedia can provide one form of visualization by using *sensory transducers* that allow users' eyes, ears, and hands to access previously unavailable objects, such as molecules. A second form of visualization, *cognitive transducers* can make intellectual entities, such as knowledge structures, visible and manipulable. Dede foresees machine-generated, simulated beings entering multimedia applications. These "knowbots" would simulate librarians and teachers, linking students to resources and showing them how to use those resources.

Future multimedia may therefore focus on creating virtual worlds, on enhancing our abilities to visualize otherwise imperceptible or unavailable worlds, and on assisting students in recognizing and using cognitive structures. Simulated beings may provide guidance in the learning process. Multimedia applications may reflect instructional models very different from what we see today, and it will be important to examine the psychosocial implications of multimedia environments (ibid.)

Possible new methods of use. Privateer (1992) describes a collaborative approach for students to acquire specific aspects of knowledge using hypertext and multimedia: when students acquire the specific knowledge, they share their learning with other members of a "core" group who, in turn, share the information they have obtained from the first group of students. This "jig-saw" puzzle approach to learning the course content frees the instructor from knowledge dissemination responsibilities and promotes the emergence of instructional roles such as coach, encourager, and resource linker.

In the future, multimedia may be used in very different ways. Certainly it has the potential to disseminate information and knowledge more effectively and efficiently than an instructor. The instructor, therefore, can find time for different learning activities, using class time to discuss implications, and to evaluate, apply, and integrate students' newly acquired knowledge. Instructors can take on the facilitator roles described above.

Probable futures for models and methods. Because multimedia is a relatively new educational tool, the variety of instructional models and methods of use are still limited. As the range of applications and extent of use in higher education expand, many new instructional models and methods of use will likely emerge. These new models and methods will make multimedia a yet more powerful tool.

Scenarios for the Future

Based on the possible and probable trends described above, two scenarios for the future of multimedia in higher education are described below. Readers can determine for themselves whether these scenarios represent a preferable future.

Scenario One: A return to Dr. Ross and her biology class. On September 10, 2003, Professor Susan Ross greets 200 new students in her introductory biology class. After introducing herself and providing each student with an opportunity to meet at least ten other students in the course, she begins to explain the course and its content. She calls up the course syllabus on a small notebook computer and the computer screen is projected onto a large screen at the front of the classroom. During her explanation of the options available for students to document what they have learned in the course, one student asks about what kinds of tests they may take if they choose a particular option. Professor Ross accesses the test given last quarter via a hypertext link and describes the nature of the test while projecting specific items on the large screen. She reminds the students that they have access to the syllabus and previous tests by connecting their individual notebook computers into the campus computer network. The connections can be made either while students are on campus or in their homes (those that are wired with fiber optic cables).

After explaining some additional aspects of course requirements, Professor Ross previews the course content. She has selected an electronic source that includes hyperlinked text, graphics, animation, still images, and full-motion video in a digital format. Each student will download the text to his/her notebook computer by plugging into the campus network; individual student accounts will be debited automatically when the downloading is completed. Professor Ross previews the text for the students in class, demonstrating the range of content by accessing each chapter from the link in the table of contents. She highlights certain aspects of various chapters, such as the three-dimensional tours of different types of cells and a sampling of the hundreds of still images that relate to specific content within the text.

Professor Ross reminds the students that laboratory activities involve a variety of simulations that can be accessed in the multimedia learning center on campus. Because these simulations benefit from a screen larger than a student's notebook computer contains, students can work in pairs in the learning center, engaging in simulated dissections, viewing specimens previously available only by using a microscope, and making decisions that demonstrate their knowledge of ecology in managing a virtual wetland. Professor Ross instructs the students to copy their files into their individual grading folders for each of the ten laboratory reports. She and her laboratory assistants can thereby grade those aspects of the reports that are not graded electronically.

Professor Ross has worked hard on developing this class, but the initial investment has paid off in freeing more of her time for consultation with individual students and small groups of students, both via e-mail and in person. The transition to a new type of teaching and learning has actually been fairly easy for her, because she started using multimedia in her classroom ten years earlier. Some of her colleagues have had a more difficult transition. They resisted using the new teaching and learning tools for several years, but research and evaluation studies indicated superior learning outcomes for the new techniques, and they realized change was required. After an initial struggle, almost everyone is comfortably using the new teaching and learning tools.

Scenario Two: A course on race, class, and gender. Jerry Jackson signed up for the individualized study version of the course on race, class, and gender at the local community college. He had the notebook computer from when he started his post-secondary education two years ago, but he quit taking classes after spring term, 2002, because he wanted to be with his new-born daughter for the first year of her life. Now that the child sleeps through the night, his taking a class seems more feasible.

Jerry registered for the class from home by accessing the community college registration center on his computer via e-mail; he'll have to pay tuition when the next Visa bill arrives. During the registration process, Jerry received the authorization number that will enable him to access the variety of resources that are digitally stored on the mainframe computer at the college. He first checked the syllabus and course requirements; the course had reasonable required content that must be covered and mastered, and a number of enrichment options appealed to Jerry.

Jerry decided to connect the computer to the high definition TV that he and wife Amanda had purchased shortly before the baby was born. He first viewed the video segment in which the course instructor welcomes students and provides a brief introduction to the course content. The instructor also provided an overview of the resources available for the course, including a hypertext book that Jerry could access on his computer, thirty one-hour videos, and six multimedia applications that could be electronically transferred to his computer and viewed on his new TV. An elaborate simulation would allow him to undergo the social experiences of various races, classes, and genders. There was also a list of other students taking the course and a suggestion that parts of the course could be more interesting if students paired up.

Jerry enjoyed the course, completing it over a four-month period by working intensely some weeks but taking time off as child care and other activities required. The hyperlinked textbook allowed him to obtain the required core knowledge quickly in some areas and to explore other topics in greater depth. He found that an acquaintance was also taking the course, and they got together for discussions about suggested issues on several occasions. Watching the videos at home was convenient and efficient. He particularly enjoyed being able to ask questions of people from different races, genders, and social classes and to receive their responses via video.

Jerry's favorite part of the course was the simulation. He could select any combination of race, class, and gender that he chose and then select to engage in a particular activity in 1922, 1962, or the present (2002). When he chose to travel as an African-American through the southern part of the United States in 1922, he experienced "Jim Crow" policies as the people that he met forced him to "know his place" as a black man. As a lower-class white female in 1962, he experienced the humiliation of seeking assistance from officials at a local welfare agency. In another use of the simulation, Jerry selected an activity and a time period and then tried to guess the particular "location" he occupied in terms of race, class, and gender.

Comment on scenarios. The real life equivalents of Susan Ross and Jerry Jackson may or may not be able to do all of what we just envisioned. If parts of these scenarios represent desired images, we can work toward creating that preferable future. If the scenarios seem probable, we can get ready to participate or be left behind.

Questions

1. What is possible in the future related to multimedia in higher education?
   — Related to hardware?
   — Related to applications?
   — Related to methods and models of use?
   What changes may occur in higher education? How will these changes affect multimedia?
   What is possible in two years? Eight years?
2. What is probable in the future related to multimedia in higher education?
   — Related to hardware?
   — Related to applications?
   — Related to methods and models of use?
   What changes are likely to occur in higher education? How will these changes affect multimedia?
   What is probable in two years? Eight years?
3. What is preferable in the future related to multimedia in higher education?
   — Related to hardware?
   — Related to applications?
   — Related to methods and models of use?
   What changes would you prefer in higher education? How will these changes affect multimedia?
   What is preferable in two years? eight years?
4. What can I do to create a preferable future related to multimedia in higher education?

Example

The future of higher education should prove interesting to everyone working in the field, but what is its relevance to one's own institution? This example describes how the concepts and information above can be applied to a specific university, in this case, the school where the authors work. Possible, probable, and preferable futures are forecast for the coming two years and eight years, emphasizing what can be done to create the future. We start with some background information.

Background Information

The University of Minnesota, Duluth, is a medium-sized comprehensive university with about 7,500 students and 300 full-time equivalent faculty members. There are now about ten multimedia applications used on campus. All of these applications can be used on either of two complete mobile multimedia systems, both of which comprise a videodisc player, CD-ROM drive, and a large hard disk; one unit is Macintosh-based and the other is an IBM Ultimedia System. Three InfoWindow systems and one two-screen Macintosh system are available through the audio-visual center in the library. The medical school has a number of Macintosh-based systems, but they are not available to other students on campus.

Multimedia is not very widely used on campus. In addition to the uses by the authors as described above, two faculty members use a videodisc and keypad in courses on anatomy and physiology, and the medical school uses videodisc applications as a learning tool to teach histology. At least twenty faculty members are aware of the capabilities of multimedia, but have not yet used this technology as a teaching or learning tool. A few people in the computer center have the necessary technical knowledge, but have not used multimedia applications for teaching.

Two Years in the Future

Possible futures. Even for two years into the future, we can envision several different possibilities. One possible outcome is continuation of the current situation. On the other hand, ten additional applications available and twenty faculty members using multimedia in their teaching would represent a dramatic change. Other possibilities lie between these two quite extreme scenarios.

Probable futures. The first scenario above—no change from current practices—is probable if nothing occurs to alter current trends. Faculty members in general are not familiar with the capabilities of multimedia, and few have the confidence to use what, for them, is a new and complicated technology. Additionally, the applications currently on campus are useful in just a few disciplines. Thus, unless something happens to change instructors perceptions, we can foresee little change.

Preferable futures. The second possible scenario—ten new applications and twenty faculty members using multimedia—represents a preferred future. It is not likely to happen, however, without something occurring to impel a change.

Creating the future. To create that preferred future, some significant action must be taken. One possibility is a workshop designed to expose faculty members to the capabilities of multimedia, to describe and demonstrate applications that exist in their disciplines, and to provide instruction on how to use multimedia as an educational tool. In addition, faculty members attending the workshop would be eligible to apply for grants to purchase multimedia applications for use with the courses they teach. Technical support for faculty members could be provided by the computer center. The workshop coupled with technical support would provide a critical mass of knowledgeable faculty members and useful applications to serve as a foundation for future development.

Eight Years in the Future

Possible futures. Almost all of the alternative futures described in the first portion of this chapter are possible in eight years and could, therefore, be in use at the University of Minnesota, Duluth. If little is done to promote multimedia on campus in the next eight years, however, teaching practices will have progressed little from their current state. On the other hand, if the technologies and applications develop rapidly and administrators and faculty members actively promote multimedia, even the more optimistic of the two scenarios described as possible in two years would seem anachronistic. Almost anything is possible in eight years.

Probable futures. The probable future on the University of Minnesota, Duluth, campus is influenced by what is generally probable for multimedia. If movement is increasingly toward digital applications, it will be difficult to buck the trend. If multimedia instruction can be provided from a distance, new competition for local students may come from afar.

Current trends suggest slow growth in the use of multimedia at the University of Minnesota, Duluth, over the next eight years. The campus has not yet embraced the latest technologies and, if this is to change, something must intervene. A probable future in eight years may find faculty in only a handful of disciplines using a mixture of videodisc-based and digital multimedia.

Preferable futures. A preferable future for multimedia on the Duluth campus might be that over half the faculty would be using some of the most advanced multimedia hardware and applications. The number of multimedia applications available for faculty and student use might rival the number of videotapes currently used. In our imagined scenarios, Professor Susan Ross would be fairly typical of the faculty members on campus, and Jerry Jackson would be one of many students using multimedia in individualized study form. Innovative models of instruction and new methods of use would be developed in response to student needs.

Creating the future. A workshop as described above still seems a reasonable first step in moving toward our preferable future. In addition, a plan for the development of multimedia capabilities that span the disciplines on campus would be most helpful. This plan would anticipate the probable future for multimedia in general and would thus meld with the trend of increasing use of digital hardware and applications. The plan would begin with an image of a preferable future with respect to multimedia use on campus and map out the steps between current practice and the preferred future. This map might include yearly workshops for faculty development, a method to monitor new developments related to multimedia, and a systematic plan for financing and purchasing multimedia hardware and software.

Guidelines

1. Remain aware of the possibilities related to multimedia in higher education.
    — Monitor hardware developments.
    — Seek relevant new applications.
    — Pursue new models and methods of using multimedia.
    — Keep your mind open about what is possible with multimedia.
2. Anticipate what is probable related to multimedia in higher education.
    Be prepared for what is probable and be in a position to use these probable futures to your advantage.
3. Develop images of the preferred future for multimedia in higher education.
    Use these images as a blueprint for attaining your goals.
4. Take action to create the future for multimedia in higher education.

Resources

All of the resources described in earlier chapters for various aspects of what is now available for multimedia also offer information on what will be possible, probable, and preferable in the future. Conferences and certain periodicals may be most up-to-date, but the time required to publish books is also reducing. Increasingly, bulletin boards and an e-mail network may provide the best information on the future of multimedia.

Conclusion

Most of this book takes a conservative approach. It suggests following the safe path, beginning with applications based on videodisc and CD-ROM, because those media are more established and stable. The approach taken and the examples provided in previous chapters focus on urging educators to try a powerful new tool that may help them become more effective teachers.

But in the words of one of the most famous sons of northeast Minnesota, Bob Dylan, "the times they are a changin'." Many forces are interacting to promote changes in higher education, and multimedia hardware capabilities and applications are most dynamic. The challenge will be to make the best use of what is now available with multimedia in higher education while at the same time preparing for the probable future and imaging and creating the preferable future.

CHAPTER 13

SUMMARY AND CONCLUSION

Brief Review

This book emphasizes use of a problem solving process for integrating multimedia in higher education as a teaching and learning tool. Consistent with problem solving principles, this instructional design process involves defining the educational problem, exploring the possible range of alternative solutions based on multimedia and other forms of instruction, examining and deciding on the best solution, and implementing and evaluating the solution selected. The key elements of each of these steps are highlighted below.

Defining the Problem

Defining problems in higher education begins with a careful examination of the setting in which multimedia may be used. This book focuses on formal instruction after secondary education has been completed. This setting is characterized by diverse societal pressures, including imperatives for increased productivity that are inherent in reduced funding. Learners in higher education increasingly reflect a greater diversity of race, class, age, and gender, and of learning styles. Higher education is charged with achieving diverse goals. And its role is complicated by a lack of consensus on what constitutes proper balance between liberal education and vocational preparation, and by the arguments concerning a dominant culture versus multicultural emphasis.

Generating Alternative Solutions

A major portion of this book focuses on understanding multimedia as a set of solutions in higher education that can help meet important learning goals for diverse groups. The capabilities of multimedia hardware are remarkable, with possible combinations of full-motion video, high-quality audio, text, graphics, and animation operating in a seamless and organized environment. Numerous instructional models are possible, including enhanced didactic presentations, directed or open exploration, simulated personal interactions, structured observation, and assessment and focused instruction. Multimedia can be used as either a teaching tool to enhance instruction in the classroom or as a learning tool to assist students in achieving education goals outside the classroom.

Hardware and instructional options can be combined to provide multimedia applications in three main ways. First, many of the more than 5,000 multimedia applications now available for purchase "off the shelf" are appropriate for use in higher education. Second, educators can develop their own applications, because the skills and resources for the development process are often present on campus. Third, applications can be repurposed; that is, new applications can be developed by modifying or re-using portions of existing applications in new and different ways. Purchasing applications is generally less expensive, but the product may not precisely address the educational problem; developing one's own application allows a focused response to the educational problem, but the process can be expensive and time consuming. Repurposing provides a middle ground.

Deciding on a Solution

Several criteria must be considered in deciding whether multimedia represents the best instructional choice for a particular situation. The instructional methods and models must be matched to the educational needs, and the instructional design and technical quality of the multimedia applications must be high if they are to be effective. Multimedia represents an appropriate alternative to traditional methods of instruction only when its advantages outweigh the disadvantages.

Implementing the Solution

A number of guidelines are important when actually using multimedia as a teaching or learning tool. Interactivity represents a key capability of multimedia, and it is important to build this advantage into the instruction from the start. Because few faculty members are currently adept at using multimedia hardware and applications, rehearsal of the instructional activities is a sound investment. Use as a teaching tool involves modeling interactive capabilities and leading students to participate in the instruction. Use as a learning tool involves providing sufficient learning stations, clear directions, and suitable support to students.

Evaluating the Solution

As a new form of instruction, it is important to evaluate multimedia in higher education. Formative evaluation involves collecting information to improve the development and use of multimedia instruction. Summative evaluation focuses on determining whether multimedia represents a more effective form of instruction in a particular setting.

Getting Started: Doing the Next Thing

As participants in higher education, each of us must start with our current knowledge and experience and then take the next step toward realizing the potential of multimedia as an instructional tool. Whether faculty members or administrators, experienced multimedia users or relative neophytes, everyone can act to foster the effective use of multimedia.

Because computers remain at the core of multimedia capabilities and instruction, it is essential to develop knowledge and skills in using this key tool. Many educators are familiar with basic uses of computers, such as for word processing, spreadsheets, and databases; those who are not will find that gaining familiarity with these applications will assist them in being more comfortable with computers and in acquiring a beginning knowledge of their capabilities. Perhaps the most important computer capability for multimedia is interactivity, and this feature can be examined by using hypertext or specific applications such as HyperCard, LinkWay, or Aldus Persuasion.

The best way to learn about multimedia is to use it. Those with limited knowledge should seek opportunities to use multimedia and thereby gain a better understanding of its capabilities. This knowledge might stimulate ideas about possible uses in educators' respective disciplines. Those who are aware of multimedia's capabilities can explore applications more thoroughly, examining the instructional models and how multimedia capabilities have been incorporated, perhaps in preparation for developing their own applications or for repurposing existing applications.

Learning to actually use multimedia as a teaching and learning tool is a challenge. Most faculty members in higher education have had little or no formal instruction in classroom techniques. They therefore rely on an informal apprenticeship, basically teaching as they were taught. This system is effective to the extent that novice faculty members incorporate the most effective methods of the various teachers they have had over the years. But the system breaks down in introducing new teaching technologies, such as multimedia: few current faculty members have been taught through multimedia and have no background for integrating this potentially powerful teaching and learning tool into their own instruction.

Faculty members must therefore be provided examples of instructors using multimedia. Workshops on campuses can demonstrate the capabilities of multimedia and the ways in which applications can be used. Faculty members can seek multimedia demonstrations at conferences in their disciplines. Teleconferences on multimedia and related topics represent an efficient method of disseminating information.

Learning to use multimedia represents a unique opportunity for sharing across disciplinary boundaries. Those educators, regardless of discipline, who know the most about multimedia and its effective use can share this information with others through campus workshops or by allowing colleagues to observe them using multimedia in classrooms and lecture halls. These demonstrations can incorporate simulated interaction, structured observation, didactic presentations, exploration, and other models of instruction while using multimedia as both a teaching and learning tool. These models and methods of use transcend disciplinary boundaries. Those educators who know relatively less can seek opportunities to expand their knowledge.

Both administrators and faculty members in higher education must be involved in expanding the effective use of multimedia. Administrators can create an atmosphere that encourages their faculties to become knowledgeable about interactive multimedia and its use and that facilitates integration of this tool into classrooms and other learning environments; sponsoring workshops and promoting travel to conferences provide examples of concrete manifestations of administrative assistance. Faculty members must seek opportunities to learn about multimedia and take risks in using the technology, realizing that any new venture involves some risk.   Both administrators and faculty members can advocate resources for education, particularly the funds for multimedia applications and hardware.

Finding the Niche for Multimedia

By systematically applying the problem solving process to its development and use, and by evaluating its effectiveness, the role of multimedia as a teaching and learning tool can be identified. The initial effort is best focused on how multimedia can help faculty members be more effective in what they are already doing; increasingly, the emphasis can shift toward reconceptualizing the teaching/learning process, including the role of multimedia and the instructor.

Finding the niche for multimedia in the current educational setting involves first a focus on the best way for faculty members to use multimedia in the classroom and for students to use multimedia outside of the classroom setting. In the classroom, multimedia applications can enrich lectures with video, stills, text, graphics, and animation. Multimedia can serve as a basis for discussion and can provide both case studies for examination and simulations for interaction. Systematic evaluation will provide information on the combination of content, learner characteristics, and instructional models by which multimedia proves most effective.

Next, faculty members can explore how multimedia will best promote student learning outside the classroom. Multimedia applications may provide advantages over books, videotapes, science laboratories, or traditional print-based library research for outside learning. The exploration and assessment model and focused instruction model may be particularly effective in assisting students. Again, evaluation provides data for enlightened decisions on the best uses of multimedia outside of the classroom.

The potential for multimedia in higher education goes far beyond marginal improvement in helping teachers teach and students learn. Multimedia can provide the impetus and the means to transform the instructional process in higher education. Just as books freed instructors from relying almost solely on transmitting information in lectures and allowed class activities to focus more on discussing and applying concepts, multimedia could free instructors to engage in roles more fitting for contemporary needs. Multimedia may prove to be more effective and efficient in transmitting certain kinds of knowledge and skills and in providing assessment of results. If instructors can turn some of their traditional roles over to multimedia, they can devote more time to roles that are increasingly essential in an information age, such as guiding students to information resources and teaching them how to use these resources in an ongoing process.

Multimedia can also play a leading role in transforming higher education. The current system was designed to meet the needs of an agricultural and industrial society, not the emerging information society. The factory model of higher education cannot effectively cope with diverse learner needs, with pressure increasing for efficiency and productivity, and with the need for knowledge and skills that go far beyond what has been traditional. As our society is transformed, multimedia can be one of the tools that higher education needs to meet its obligations in the age of information.

The potential of multimedia in higher education remains largely unfulfilled. Given its current capabilities and numerous options for the future, the possible applications for multimedia seem almost unlimited. If trends continue, the capabilities of multimedia hardware and applications may continue to outpace the abilities of most instructors to use them to full advantage. The preferable future for multimedia in higher education must first be imagined and clarified. We can then work cooperatively toward realizing the preferable future in which multimedia fills its proper niche in a transformed teaching/learning process that better addresses tomorrow's educational problems.

PART 5

Resources

Part 5 provides information about a number of resources for multimedia in higher education. The following is a brief description of the types of materials in each section.

A number of resources are listed in the appendix, providing telephone numbers of organizations, publications, and vendors mentioned in the "Resources" sections of various chapters. The appendix also contains a short bibliographic list of relevant books and articles not included in the references.

The "Glossary" includes definitions of a number of terms related to multimedia.

"References" comprises all the materials, including books and articles, cited in the text.

The "Index" provides assistance in finding where specific topics are covered in the text.

Appendix

Resources

NOTE: The telephone numbers are accurate at the time of printing. In the field of computers and multimedia, numbers change frequently. Please contact information if the number is inaccurate.

Examples of Journals and Periodicals

Academic Computing	800-531-3227
CD-ROM Professional	800-543-4383
Chronicle of Higher Education	202-466-1080
Computer Teacher	503-346-4414
Curriculum Product News	203-322-1300
EDUCOM Review	202-872-4200
Educational Technology	201-871-4007
Educational Technology Research and Development	202-347-7834
Educational Technology Systems	800-457-6812
Electronic Learning	212-505-4940
Instruction Delivery Systems	703-347-0055
Journal of Educational Multimedia and Hypermedia Journal of Multimedia Computing Media and Methods	212-563-3501
Multimedia & Videodisc Monitor	703-730-4011
Multimedia Review	203-226-6967
NewMedia	(Fax) 413-637-4343
T.H.E. Journal	714-730-4011
Videodisc Compendium for Education and Teaching	612-639-3973

Examples of Professional Organizations

Association for Educational Communications and Technology	202-347-7634
Association for Supervision and Curriculum Development	703-549-1403
Institute for the Transfer of Technology to Education	703-838-6219
Interactive Multimedia Association	410-626-1380
International Communications Industry Association	703-273-7200
International Society for Technology in Education	503-346-4414
International Television Association	214-869-1112
National Demonstration Laboratory	202-707-4157
Nebraska Videodisc Group Society for Applied Learning Technology	800-457-6812
Tech 2000	202-842-0500
Technology Resources Center	202-219-1699

Examples of Vendors and Distributors

ABC News InterActive 800-524-2481
Advanced Digital Systems 800-888-5244
Agency for Instructional Technology 800-457-4509
AIMS Media 800-578-8690
Aldus Corporation 800-332-5387
Allen Communication 800-325-7050
Apple Computer 408-996-1010
Associates for Advancement of
   Computing in Education 804-973-3987
Asymetrix Corporation 800-448-6543
Authorware, Incorporated 800-445-5415
Bureau of Electronic Publishing 800-828-4766
Canon U. S. A. 800-221-3333, X313
Center for Interactive Multimedia for
   Education and Training 206-676-3516
Claris Corporation 800-544-8554, X98
Compton's New Media 619-929-2500
Confer. 800-801-0040
Coronet/MTI Film & Video. 800-777-8100
Digital Archives Collection 800-782-4479
Eastman Kodak Company 716-726-4000
Educational Resources 800-624-2926
Educorp 800-843-9497
Eiki International, Incorporated. 800-242-3454
Emerging Technology Consultants 612-639-3973
Encyclopedia Britannica Educational Corp. 800-554-9862
Farallon Computing 520-596-9000
Future Systems, Incorporated 703-241-1799
General Television Network 313-548-2500
Hartley Courseware. 800-247-1380
Highsmith 800-558-2110
HyperGlot Software Company 800-726-5087
IBM Corporation (Multimedia & Education) 800-426-9402
Image Entertainment 818-407-9100
InFocus Systems, Incorporated 800-327-7231
Intellimation. 800-346-8355
Interactive Image Technologies 416-361-0323
Laser Learning Technologies 800-722-3505
LucasArts Learning (Coronet/MTI) 800-777-8100
MacroMind, Incorporated 800-945-4061
MECC 800-685-MECC
Mecklermedia 203-226-6967
Miami-Dade Community. 305-347-2158
Microsoft Corporation 206-882-8080
National Geographic Society 800-368-2728
NEC Technologies, Incorporated 800-NEC-INFO
nVIEW Corporation. 800-736-8439
Online Computer Systems, Incorporated 800-832-2722
Optical Data Corporation 800-524-2481
Panasonic Corporation 800-524-0864
PC Zone 800-448-8892

Philips Interactive Media. 800-223-4432
Pioneer Communications of America 800-243-2015
Radius Incorporated 800-452-5524
RasterOps Corporation 800-SAY-COLOR
Ricoh Corporation 800-955-FILE
Sharp Electronics Corporation 800-BE-SHARP
SilverPlatter Information Systems 800-343-0064
Sony Corporation of America. 800-472-SONY
Stokes Imaging Services 512-458-2201
3M Company 800-227-2547
Technidisc Incorporated 800-727-8700
The Discovery Channel   301-986-1999
Tiger Media 213-721-8282
Toshiba America, Incorporated 713-583-3000
Videodiscovery, Incorporated 800-548-3472
VideoLogic, Incorporated 617-494-0530
VideoNetworking Link Systems. 800-237-LINK
Voyager Company. 310-451-1383
Warner NewMedia 800-593-6354
Wayzata Technology 800-735-7321
Wilson Learning Corporation. 800-328-7937
Ztek 800-247-1603

Books and articles not listed in the references

Ambron, S. & Hooper, K. (1988). *Interactive multimedia: Visions of multimedia for developers, educators and information users*. Redmond, WA: Microsoft Press.

Ambron, S. & Hooper, K. (1990). *Learning with interactive multimedia*. Redmond, WA: Microsoft Press.

Ambrose, D.W. (1991). The effects of hypermedia on learning: A literature review. *Educational Technology, 31*, 12, 51-55.

Bove, T. & Rhodes, C. (1990). *Macintosh multimedia handbook*. Carmel, IN: Que Corporation.

Burger, J. (1993). *Deskstop multimedia bible*. Reading, MA: Addison-Wesley.

Dede, C. (1993). Trends and forecasts. *EDUCOM Review, 28*, 6, 35-38

Gagne, R.M. (1987). *Instructional technology: Foundations*. Hillsdale, NJ: Erlbaum Associates.

Greer, M. (1992). *Tools and techniques for instructional designers and developers*. Englewood Cliffs, NJ: Educational Technology Publications.

Haynes, G.R. (1989). *Opening minds: The evolution of videodiscs and interactive learning*. Falls Church, VA: Future Systems.

Hefzallah, I.M., Editor (1990). *The new learning and telecommunications technologies: Their potential applications in education*. Springfield, IL: Charles C. Thomas.

Imke, S. (1991). *Interactive video management and production*. Englewood Clifs, NJ: Educational Technology Publications.

Interactive Video Industry Association (1990). *The power of multimedia*. Glenview, IL: Interactive Multimedia Association.

Laff, N.S. (1989). Adventures in the gray zone: Critical/creative thinking and how to structure the personal meaning of education. *Research and teaching in developmental education, 6*, 1, 5-20.

Lovell-Troy, L. & Eickmann, P. (1992). *Course design for college teachers*. Englewood Cliffs, NJ: Educational Technology Publications.

Lyons, P. (1992). *Thirty-five lesson formats: A sourcebook of instructional alternatives*. Englewood Cliffs, NJ: Educational Technology Publications.

McBeath, R.J., Editor (1992). *Instructing and evaluating in higher education: A guidebook for planning learning outcomes*. Englewood Cliffs, NJ: Educational Technology Publications.

Nickerson, R. & Zodhiates, P.P. (9188). *Technology in education: Looking toward 2020*. Hillsdale, NJ: Lawrence Erlbaum Associates.

Nix, D. & Spiro, R. (1990). *Cognition, education, & multimedia: Exploring ideas in high technology*. Hillsdale, NJ: Lawrence Erlbaum Asociates.

Rathbone, A. (1994). *Multimedia and CD-ROM for dummies*. San Mateo, CA: IDG Books Worldwide.

Schwier, R. (1988). *Interactive video*. Englewood Cliffs, NJ: Educational Technology Publications.

Tway, L. (1992). *Welcome to multimedia*. New York: MIS Press.

Wodaski, R. (1994). *Multimedia Madness (Deluxe edition)*. Indianapolis: SAMS Publishing.

Glossary

analog—form of knowledge representation based on continuously varying color or tone; contrasted with digital (binary)

ASCII—system used to code alphabetic, numerical, and other symbols into binary codes used in computing

assessment and focused instruction—instructional design model in which a multimedia application is used to test a learner's knowledge of a particular topic and to direct the student to an appropriate level of instruction or remediation

audience analysis (learner analysis)—complete description of the intended users of an application, as to demographics, skills, attitudes, concepts, educational level, etc.

audio mixer—device that combines and blends several sound inputs into one or two outputs simultaneously

audio track—tracks on videotape or disc that record the audio signal; systems with two separate audio tracks can be used for stereo or two independent signals

authoring language—high-level computer program that translates the instructions into a language resembling everyday English

authoring system—prepackaged courseware designed to help authors lacking elaborate programming skills create instructional programs

baud—measure of data transmission speed roughly equivalent to the number of signals per second; often each signal equals a data bit

binary notation—counting system that uses only two digits, 0 and 1, and a base-two number system; used to represent numerals, letters, symbol "off and on"; this system can be recorded on a magnetic storage medium

bit—binary digit, either a 0 or a 1, which is the smallest unit in computer information handling

bit-mapped graphics—image created on computer screen by either turning dots on or off or changing the dots' color values

boot—process of turning on a computer and bringing its operating system to function

branch—path chosen from several alternatives; often used in Level Three interactive multimedia applications

button—icon, piece of text, or part of graphic that signals the beginning of a link (branching) or that initiates some action

byte—basic unit of data storage; eight bits represent one byte

card—computing term used synonymously with "board;" one screen of information in a stack (used in Hypercard)

CAV (constant angular velocity)—laser videodisc format that holds 54,000 still frames and 30 minutes of linear video on each side of the disc; frames individually addressable

CD-I (compact-disc interactive)—optical disc that can handle varieties of media: 7,800 video still frames, 2 hours of top-quality audio, 17 hours of narration, 150,000 pages of text and graphics; self-contained system that displays interactive stills and motion clips controlled by a simple handset

CD-ROM—small optical disc that stores data in digital format: 5,000 real life images, 150,000 pages of text and graphics; stores still-frame video, audio, data, and computer code; roughly equivalent to the storage capacity of 500 floppy disks

CD-ROM XA—medium that incorporates audio and graphics from both CD-I and CD-ROM formats

chapter—segment of a computer program or interactive video program that is independent and self-contained; portion of video on a CLV format videodisc

chip—device in which microscopic electronic circuitry is printed photographically on the surface of semiconductor material (silicon)

chooser—part of system that allows the user to select and control connected peripherals (used on the Macintosh system)

C language—powerful language used by computer programmers for complex interactive media programs

clipboard—part of computer member dedicated to holding text and/or graphics that have been copied or cut; information from clipboard can then be pasted into application

CLV (constant linear velocity)—long-play videodiscs that offer a good medium for entertainment and that now work interactively with Pioneer 8000

compiler—utility for converting a program written in a high-level language to machine language

computer programmer—participant in the multimedia production team who converts Level Three flowchart into the branching needed for the instructional program

CPU (central processor)—"brain" of the computer in which instructions, calculations, and data manipulation take place

cursor—flashing shape on computer screen that indicates where information may be next entered

cut-and-paste—transfer of information from one location to another (in a computer program)

database—file of information that users may use or change as part of a larger project or program

digital—data that is generated or translated into patterns of discrete, fixed values; digital information refers to computer-based technology that uses binary notation

disc (or disk), diskette—flat circular plastic plate that can be used to record and replay either analog or digital information (*see* videodisc and CD-ROM)

DVI (digital video interactive)—medium that uses digital compression and decompression to store digitized video and audio on a CD-ROM, digital tape, or large-capacity computer hard drive

expert system—interactive program that solves problems based on a "knowledge base" created by experts in a field; operates on users' responses to a set of questions and a system of "if-then" rules

exploration—instructional design model in which learners move through a multimedia application in an individualized, exploratory manner

field dominance—field, even or odd, on which any given frame begins; important to establish which field starts a sequence when editing

flowchart—diagram representing a computer program in graphic form; basic elements are identified with specific shapes in computer flowcharting

frame number—location of each frame on a videodisc; frames are numbered consecutively from 1 to 54,000.

freeze frame—single frame from a strip of moving footage held motionless on screen

graphics (PC)—text or pictorial artwork created with graphics software and stored on PC hard disk or CD-ROM

graphics (Video)—text or pictorial artwork created by various means and then recorded on tape and pressed onto a videodisc

hard disk—magnetic disk with great storage capacity often sealed within a computer to provide large memory

HyperCard—software construction kit that is often used to create hypertext/hypermedia applications (Macintosh)

hypermedia—software programs that consist of related text, graphics, audio files, and video clips; users access these through various search strategies

hypertext—software program that consists of networks of related text files; users access through various search strategies

instructional designer—participant in the multimedia production team who designs the instructional goals, strategies, and content flow of an interactive multimedia program (based on learner analysis and identified objectives)

interactive multimedia (hypermedia)—computer program that combines text, graphics, video, audio, and/or animation in a way that involves learner response

interactive video (IV)—convergence of video and computer technology in which the two run in tandem under the control of the user

interactivity—program that takes the user's actions into account and responds accordingly

interactivity, levels of (or separately under "L": Level One, Level Two, etc)—describes the interactivity in videodisc players; Level One includes remote control, freeze frame, forward and reverse motion, quick scan, slow motion, and step frame replay; Level Two, with its own microprocessor, offers multiple choice, branching, and scorekeeping; Level Three includes a videodisc player linked to an external computer with high versatility of any interactive configuration

laser—acronym of Light Amplification by Stimulated Emission of Radiation; uses the energy of excited atoms to produce an intense beam of light (electromagnetic radiation); used with optical media such as videodisc

laser videodisc—name used to describe the reflective optical videodisc

learning style—personal affective, cognitive, and environmental adaptations that influence the learning process

learning tool, multimedia—multimedia application that involves the learner(s) at a workstation using the instructional program in a self-directed manner

light pen—remote control device that allows the user to write or draw on the screen of a monitor

manager—participant in the multimedia team who organizes the tasks of the group and facilitates positive interactions among members

mastering—stage in production of a videodisc in which a master disc is created

megabyte—measure of data storage equivalent to 1,024 kilobytes; 500 pages of text equivalency

mouse—remote control device which can be guided by hand on a tablet or other surface to direct the cursor on the computer screen

MPC—hardware and software systems, which include support for CD-ROM, digitized audio and video, and high resolution graphics, and which use a Windows environment on PC equipment

MS-DOS—acronym for Microsoft Disk Operating System; operating system for (IBM or compatible) personal computers

multimedia—systems that integrate video, text, graphics, and audio, often through combining a computer with an optical technology unit (videodisc player, CD player)

Multimedia Extensions (PC)—software (by Microsoft) providing IBM PCs and compatibles multimedia capabilities

needs analysis—description of the needs of the intended users of an instructional program (see audience analysis)

NLS (oN Line System)—hypertext/teleconferencing system

NTSC—television color standard with a 525-line screen and a running speed of 30 frames per second; used in the United States, Canada, and Asia (*see* also PAL)

operating system—software that directs program execution and access to peripheral units in a personal computer system

optical disc—software based on the idea that information can be translated into physical impressions on a disc and read by a laser beam that decodes the signals into video, text, graphics, and audio

PAL—television and video color standard with a 625-line screen and 25 frames per second; standard used in most of Europe, Africa, Australia, and South America (*see* also NTSC)

PC-VCR—videocassette recorder that can be controlled by a personal computer via a serial cable to support interactive video, video databases, and computer-controlled editing

peripherals—equipment controlled by the computer but physically independent of it

pixel—abbreviation of "picture element;" one of thousands of points of light and color that make up a computer screen

post production—activity in videodisc production that includes the editing stage and the preparation of the tape for reproduction as an interactive tape or disc

premastering—production stage in which the master tape is checked and prepared for transfer onto the master disc, such as a videodisc

production expert—participant in the multimedia production team who determines how best to portray each aspect of the visual and audio components

QuickTime—multimedia technology that supports the storage and distribution (through local networks) of video motion, stills, and audio information on a Macintosh computer

RAM (random access memory)—part of computer's memory that can both read and write information and that can be updated or amended by the programmer or user

random access—ability to access information by direct address (frame number) as opposed to a linear search of information

repurposing—use of an authoring system that accesses an optical disc's audio, visual, text, and graphics and combines them in new ways

RGB—red-green-blue; a high-quality color screen

scrapbook—utility program that allows the user to store images and text for insertion into a program at a later time (Macintosh)

search—use of computer or keypad to access specific information stored on optical disc in a rapid, random process

SECAM—television standard in France and a few other countries

simulated personal interaction—instructional design model in which the multimedia application contains a case study or situation in which the learners participate and in which they influence interactions

step frame—ability to move through a video sequence frame by frame, forward or backward by using a control device

still frame—graphic of any kind that is presented as a single, static image rather than as moving footage; economical storage of still frames is a strength of videodiscs

structured observation—instructional design model in which the multimedia application contains set guidelines for observing the segments in the program

storyboard—written plan that illustrates how the video, audio, text, and graphics components of a multimedia program will be combined

SuperCard—collection of cards; HyperCard-like construction kit

teaching tool, multimedia—use of multimedia application where the instructor selectively uses specific aspects of an application to enhance the presentation

teleconferencing—communication over telephone lines or satellite broadcasting that combines voice with still frames or motion video

three/two pulldown—method used to reconcile PAL (24 frames per second) video to NTSC (30 frames per second) video

videodisc—medium that stores information in analog fashion; "mastered" with pits that contain audio and video information which is then read with a laser beam; decoded data is presented on standard television sets or computer monitors

videodisc interface—combination of hardware and software that makes it possible to control a videodisc player by a computer

video-enhanced didactic presentation—instructional design model that selectively uses text, audio, graphics, and video to present content in a direct and straightforward manner

virtual reality—system that allows the user to interact vicariously with synthetic scenes through use of computer, datagloves, helmets, or joysticks

window—rectangular part of a computer screen that acts as a display independent of the ongoing program

Windows (Microsoft)—graphics interface software operating system providing use of multimedia and other applications for IBM PC or compatible computers

References

Adams, D., Carlson, H., & Hamm, Mary (1990). *Cooperative learning & educational media: Collaborating with technology and each other.* Englewood Cliffs, NJ: Education Technology Publications.

Adelman, Clifford (1989). *Cultural literacies in the college curriculum: The records of a generation.* Washington, DC: Department of Education. (ERIC Document Reproduction Service No. ED 318377).

Altbach, Philip (1991). Patterns in higher education development: Toward the year 2000. *Prospects, 21,* 4, 189-203.

Amara, R (1981). The futures field: Searching for definitions and boundaries. *The Futurist,* February, 25-29.

Anderson, C. & Veljkov, M. (1990). *Creating interactive multimedia: A practical guide.* Glenview, IL: Scott, Foresman.

Arch, C. L. (1994). *Authoring interactive multimedia.* Boston: AP Professional (for IBM).

Arwady, J. & Gayeski, D. (1989). *Using video: Interactive and linear designs.* Englewood Cliffs, NJ: Educational Technology Publications.

Bailey, G. D. (1992). Wanted: A road map for understanding integrated learning systems. *Educational Technology, 31,* 9, 3-5.

Barron, A. & Baumbach, D. (1990a). Three ways to get hyper. *Proceedings of the Eighth Interactive Instruction Delivery Conference.* Warrenton, VA: Society for Applied Learning Technologies.

Barron, A. & Baumbach, D. (1990b). A CD-ROM tutorial: Training for a new technology. *Educational Technology, 30,* 1, 20-23.

Barton, P. E. & Kirsch, I. S. (1990). *Workplace competencies: The need to improve literacy and employment readiness.* Washington, D C: U. S. Department of Education.

Banathy, B. H. (1991). *Systems design of education: A journey to create the future.* Englewood Cliffs: NJ: Educational Technology Publications.

Bayard-White, C. (1986). *An introduction to interactive video.* London, UK: Council for Eductional Technology for the National Interactive Video Centre.

Bergman, R. & Moore, T. (1990). *Managing interactive video/ multimedia projects.* Englewood Cliffs, NJ: Educational Technology Publications.

Bloom, A. (1987). *The closing of the American mind.* New York: Simon and Schuster.

Bonwell, C. & Eiser, J. A. (1991). *Active learning: Creating excitement in the classroom.* Washington, DC: George Washington University (ERIC Document Reproduction Service No. ED 340272).

Borco, J. (1986). An analysis of evaluations of interactive video. *Educational Technology, 16,* 5, 7-17.

Brady, P. & Santo, P. (1992). *The implications of the remote area teacher education program for tertiary distance education in Queensland, Australia.* Paris, France: International Council for the Education of Teachers 30th World Assembly.

Burger, J. (1994). New directions in authoring, *New Media, 4,* 5, 44-50.

Bureau of the Census (1991). *Statistical abstract of the United States 1991.* Washington, DC: United States Government Printing Office.

Carlson, H. (1991). Learning style and program design in interactive multimedia, *Educational Technology Research and Development, 39,* 3, 41-48.

Carlson, H. & Falk, D. (1991). Effectiveness of interactive videodisc instructional programs in elementary teacher education. *Journal of Educational Technology Systems, 19,* 2, 151-163.

Carlson, H. L. & Falk, D. R. (1990). Interactive learning models using videodiscs in college and inservice instruction for human service professionals. *Computers in Human Services, 7,* 3/4, 277-294.

Carlson, H. L. & Falk, D. R. (1989). Effective use of interactive videodisc instruction in understanding and implementing cooperative group learning with elementary pupils in social studies and social education. *Theory and Research in Social Education, 17,* 241-258.

Carlson, H. L. & Nierengarten, M. (1989). Subject matter experts: A key to designing interactive videodiscs. *Educational Technology, 29,* 10, 46-48.

Casement, W. (1987). Bloom and the great books. *Journal of General Education, 39,* 1, 1-9.

Clark, R. E. (1989). Current progress and future directions for research in instructional technology. *Educational Technology Research and Development, 37,* 1, 57-66.

Daynes, R. (1987). *Designing and developing interactive videodiscs.* Germantown, MD: Pacific Interactive MIS, subsidiary of Online Computer Systems.

DeBloois, M. L (1982). *Videodisc/microcomputer courseware design.* Englewood Cliffs, NJ: Educational Technology Publications.

DeBloois, M. L. (1988). *Use and effectiveness of videodisc training: A status report.* Falls Church, VA: Future Systems Inc.

Dede, C. J. (1992). The future of multimedia: Bridging to virtual worlds. *Educational Technology, 32,* 5, 54-60.

Dick, W. & Carey, L. (1985) *The systematic design of instruction (2nd Ed.).* Glenview, IL: Scott, Foresman.

Drake, S. (1987). Does IVI really work? *Data Training,* May, 16-19.

Falk, D. R. (1993). A little bit of this, a little bit of that: The interactive process of multimedia repurposing. *Proceedings of Interactive Multimedia '93.* Warrenton, VA: Society for Applied Learning Technology.

Falk, D. R. (1991). Designing from both ends: The interactive process of repurposing videodiscs. *Journal of Interactive Instruction Development, 4,* 1, 13-20.

Falk, D. R. (1990). The effectiveness of alternate models of videodisc applications in human service and teacher education. *Journal of Interactive Instruction Development, 3,* 2, 9-15.

Falk, D. R. (1988). Using interactive video to increase sensitivity to human diversity. *Conference Proceedings.* Brighton, UK: British Interactive Video Association.

Falk, D. R. (1980). Futuristics and the professional education of social workers, in Redd, K. and Harkins, A. (eds), *Education: A Time for Decisions*. Washington, DC: World Future Society.

Falk, D. R. & Carlson, H. L. (1992). Learning to teach with multimedia. *T.H.E. Journal, 20*, 2, 96-100.

Falk, D. R. & Carlson, H. L. (1991). Evaluating the effectiveness of multimedia applications in human service and teacher education. *Multimedia Review, 2*, 3, 12-18.

Falk, D. R. & Carlson, H. L. (1990). Using videodisc applications to increase sensitivity to cultural diversity among human service students. *Computers in Human Services, 7*, 3/4, 265-276.

Falk, D. R. & Carlson, H. L. (1987). Using videodisc programs on understanding groups in a university setting. *Proceedings of the 1986 National Videodisc Symposium on Education*. Lincoln, NE: University of Nebraska.

Flagg, B. (1990). *Formative evaluation for educational technologies*. Hillsdale, NJ: Lawrence Erlbaum Associates.

Floyd, S. & Floyd, B. (1982). *Handbook of interactive video*. White Plains, NY: Knowledge Industry Publications.

Foa, L. J. (1989). Power and potential: The university and instructional design. In Johnson, K. & Foa, L., editors. *Instructional design: New alternatives for effective education and training*. New York: Macmillan.

Galbreath, J. (1992a). The educational buzzword of the 1990s: Multimedia, or is it hypermedia, or interactive multimedia, or . . .? *Educational Technology, 32*, 4, 15-19.

Galbreath, J. (1992b). The coming of digital desktop media. *Educational Technology, 32*, 6, 27-32.

Goals for education: Challenge 2000. Atlanta, GA: Southern Regional Education Board. (ERIC Document Reproduction Service No. ED 301966).

Helsel, S. K. (1990). *Interactive optical technologies in education and training: Market and trends*. Westport, CT: Meckler.

Helsel, S. K. (1992). Virtual reality and education. *Educational Technology, 32*, 5, 38-42.

Henderson, R. W. & Lindesman, E. M. (1989). Interactive videodisc instruction in precalculus. *Journal of Educational Technology Systems, 17*, 2, 91-101.

Hsu, H. (1990). *The multicultural urban community college: Conflict and achievement*. San Francisco: International Conference on Leadership Development for the League of Innovation. (ERIC Reproduction Document No. 322966)

Husen, T. (1991). The idea of the university: Changing roles, current crises, and future challenges. *Prospects, 21*, 4, 171-188.

Iuppa, N. (1990). *A practical guide to interactive video design*. White Plains, NY: Knowledge Industry Publications.

Iuppa, N. & Anderson, K. (1988). *Advanced interactive video design*. White Plains, NY: Knowledge Industry Publications.

Johnson, K. & Foa, L., editors (1989). *Instructional design: New alternatives for effective education and training*, New York: Macmillan.

Jonassen, D. H. (1985). Interactive lesson design: A taxonomy. *Educational Technology, 25*, 6, 7-16.

Kaye, T. & Rumble, G. (1991). Open universities: A comparative approach. *Prospects, 21*, 4, 214-226.

Kearsley, G. (1992). Multimedia projects: Issues and applications. *Journal of Educational Multimedia and Hypermedia, 1*, 103-110.

Kemp, J. E. (1985). *The instructional design process*. New York: Harper & Row.

King, P. M., Kitchener, K. S., Davison, M. L., Parker, D. A. & Wood, P. K. (1983). The justification of beliefs in young adults: A longitudinal study. *Human Development, 26*, 106-116.

Kolb, D. A. (1981). Learning styles and disciplinary differences. In A. W. Chickering (ed.) *The modern American college*. San Francisco: Jossey-Bass.

Kolb, D. A. (1985). *The learning style inventory*. Boston: McBer and Company.

Leshlin, C. B., Pollock, J. & Reigeluth, C. M. (1992). *Instructional design strategies and tactics*. Englewood Cliffs, NJ: Educational Technology Publications.

Littlejohn, A. C. & Parker, J. M. (1988). Compact disks in an academic library: Developing an evaluation methodology. *Laserdisk Professional, 1*, 1, 36-43.

Lucas, L. (1992). Interactivity: What is it and how do you use it? *Journal of Educational Multimedia and Hypermedia, 1*, 1, 7-10.

Marlino, M. R. (1990). Evaluating multimedia: Lessons learned from the past. *Multimedia Review: Journal of Multimedia Computing*, Fall, 14-18.

Martel, L. D. (1988). From a nation at risk to a nation of promise: The role of continuing higher education in the 21st century. *Journal of Continuing Higher Education, 3*, 3-14.

McCarthy, B. (1986). *The hemispheric mode indicator*. Barrington, IL: Excel, Inc.

McCarthy, B. (1990). Using the 4Mat system to bring learning styles to schools. *Educational Technology, 48*, 2, 31-37.

McIntosh, S. (1990). *The Multimedia Producer's Legal Survival Guide*. Multimedia Computing Corporation: Santa Clara, CA.

McNeil, B. J. & Nelson, K. R. (1991). Meta-analyses of interactive video instruction: A 10-year review of achievement effects. *Journal of Computer-Based Instruction, 18*, 1, 1-6.

Meng, Guang-ping (1989). *Learning in school-run enterprises: Innovative methods of technical and vocational education*. Bonn, Germany: Federal Ministry of Education and Science Report of the UNESCO International Symposium, 46-49.

Miles, S. L. (1986). *The vocational-liberal arts controversy: Looking backwards*. Sugar Grove, IL: Waubonsee Community College (ERIC Document Reproduction Service No. ED 292496).

Miller, M. (1992). Multimedia. *PC Magazine*. March 31, 112-123.

Moore, W. G. (1983). *The measure of intellectrual development: A brief review*. Farmville, MD: Center for the Applications of Developmental Instruction.

Moore, W. S. (1990). *Beyond content: Re-framing questions of student learning*. Olympia, WA: Student Outcomes Research Institute. (ERIC Reproduction Document No. ED 322867).

Morse, S. W. (1989). *Renewing civic capacity: Preparing college students for service and citizenship*. Washington, DC: The George Washington University (ERIC Document Reproduction No. ED 320524).

Multimedia Source Guide 94-95 (1994). Special Supplement to *T.H.E. Journal*, May.

Page, M. (1990). *Active learning: Historical and contemporary perspectives.* Amherst, MA: University of Massachusetts. (ERIC Document Reproduction No. ED 338389).

Pelikan, J. (1992). *The idea of the university: A re-examination.* New Haven, CT: Yale University Press.

Perlmuter, M. (1991). *Producer's guide to interactive videodisc.* White Plains, NY: Knowledge Industry Publications.

Perry, W. G. (1970). *Forms of intellectual and ethical development in the college years.* New York: Holt, Rinehart, and Winston.

Phillips, T. L., Hannafin, M. J. & Tripp, S. D. (1988). The effects of practice and orienting behavior on learning from interactive video. *Educational Communication and Technology Journal, 36,* 1, 93-102.

Privateer, P. & MacCrate, C. (1992). Odyssey project: A search for learning solutions. *T.H.E. Journal, 20,* 3, 76-80.

Raitt, David I. (1989). *Evaluating CD-ROMs: An observational perspective.* New York: National Online Meeting. (ERIC Reproduction Document No. ED 322925).

re:act (1984). Viewing goes up. *Action for Children's Television Magazine, 13,* 4.

Reeves, T. C. (1989). The role, methods, and worth of evaluation in instructional design. In Johnson, K. & Foa, L., editors, *Instructional design: New alternatives for effective education and training.* New York: Macmillan.

Reeves, T. C. (1986). Research and evaluation models for the study of interactive video. *Journal of Computer Based Instruction, 13,* 4, 102-106.

Reigeluth, C. M. (1983). *Instructional Design: Theories and Models.* Hillsdale, NJ: Lawrence Erlbaum Associates.

Reitz, Charles (1988). *Bennett, Bloom and Boyer: Toward a critical discussion.* Kansas City, MO: Southwest College Humanities Association. (ERIC Document Reproduction Service No. ED 301306).

Rendall, Heather (1991). *Making the most of micro-computers. Technology in language learning series.* London, UK: Centre for Information of Language Teaching and Research. (ERIC Reproduction Document No. ED 339240).

Rendon, L. (1989). *The lie and the hope. Making higher education a reality for at-risk students.* Washington, DC: American Association for Higher Education. (ERIC Document Reproduction Service No. ED 308747).

Rice, R. E. (1991). *Rethinking what it means to be a scholar.* Forthcoming Carnegie Report. (ERIC Document Reproduction No. ED 333938).

Riskin, S. R. (1990). *Teaching through interactive multi-media programming. A new philosophy of the social sciences and a new epistemology of creativity.* (ERIC Reproduction Document No. ED 327133)

Sales, G. C. (1989). Repurposing: Authoring tools for the videodisc. *Computing Teacher, 16,* 9, 12-14.

Savenye, W. C. (1992). Instructional interactive video—what works? *Young Academic Monograph.* Washington, DC: National Society for Performanace and Instruction.

Sayre, S. & Montgomery, R. (1990). The feasibility of low cost videodisc repurposing. *TDC Technical Report No. 9.* St. Paul, MN: Technology Development Center, Minnesota Extension Service.

Schmidt, W. D. (1992). Improving media production design skills through the use of a design analysis checklist. *Tech Trends,* 47-50.

Schwier, R. & Misanchuk, E. R. (1993). *Interactive multimedia instruction.* Englewood Cliffs, NJ: Educational Technology Publications.

Scriven, M. (1967). The methodology of evaluation. In Tyler, R., Gagne, R. & Scriven, M. (eds.), *Perspectives of curriculum evaluation* (39-83). Chicago: Rand McNally.

Scott, T., Cole, M. & Engel, M. (1992). Computers and education: A cultural constructivist perspective. In *Review of Research in Education, 18.* Washington, DC: American Educational Research Association.

Seels, B. & Glasgow, Z. (1990). *Exercises in instructional design.* Columbus, OH: Merrill.

Slee, E. J. (1989). A review of research on interactive video. In M. R. Simonson & D. Frey (eds), *Eleventh annual proceedings of selected research paper presentations at the 1989 annual convention of the Association for Education Communications and Technology in Dallas, Texas,* 150-166. Ames, IA: Iowa State University.

Sloane, H. N., Gordon, H. M., Gunn, C. & Michelsen, V. N. G. (1989). *Evaluating educational software.* New York: Prentice Hall.

Smith, S. G. & Jones, L. L. (1986). The video laboratory—a new element in teaching chemistry. *Perspectives in Computing, 6,* 2, 20-26.

Spring, M. (1991) Informating with virtual reality. In Helsel, S. K. & Ruth, J. P., eds., *Virtual reality: Theory, practice, and promise.* Westport, CT: Meckler.

Swift, J. S. (1990). *Social consciousness and career awareness: Emerging link in higher education.* Washington, DC: Association for the Study of Higher Education. (ERIC Reproduction Document No. ED 334940.)

Tohme, G. (1990). *The university and literacy.* Geneva, Switzerland: International Bureau of Education. (ERIC Document Reproduction Service No. ED 321041).

Tucker, S. A. & Dempsey, J. V. (1991). *Semiotic criteria for evaluating instructional hypermedia.* Chicago: American Educational Research Association. (ERIC Document Reproduction Service No. ED 337155).

UNESCO (1974). *Recommendation concerning education for international understanding, cooperation and peace and education relating to human rights and fundamental freedoms.* Paris, France: General Conference Eighteenth Session.

UNESCO (1991). *World Education Report, 1991.* Paris, France: United Nations Educational, Scientific and Cultural Organization.

Van Cleaf, D. (1988). Planning models: Two alternatives to Hunter. *Educational Considerations, 15,* 3-15.

Vaughan, T. (1993). *Multimedia: Making it work.* New York: Osborne McGraw-Hill.

Waterous, F. B. (1989). From Salomon's house to the land-grant college: Practical arts education and the utopian vision of progress. *Educational Theory, 39,* 4, 359-72.

Williams, D. & Colby, A. (1991). *The community college role in achieving adult literacy.* Los Angeles: ERIC Clearinghouse for Junior Colleges. (ERIC Reproduction Document No. ED 333951).

Wlodkowski, R. J. (1989). In Johnson, K. & Foa, L., eds., *Instructional design: New alternatives for effective education and training.* New York: Macmillan.

Wodaski, R. (1994). *Multimedia madness (Deluxe edition).* Indianapolis: SAMS Publishing.

Wolf, D., Bixby, J., Glenn, J. & Gardner, H. (1991). To use their minds well: Investigating new forms of student assessment. In Grant, G., *Review of Research in Education, 17,* 31-74. Washington, DC: American Educational Research Association.

Wolfgram, D. E. (1994). *Creating multimedia presentations.* Indianapolis: Que Publications.

Additional References

Falk, Dennis R.(1993). A Little Bit of This, a Little Bit of That: The Interactive Process of Multimedia Repurposing. *Proceedings of Interactive Multimedia '93.* Warrenton, VA: Society for Applied Learning Technology.

McIntosh, S. (1990). *The Multimedia Producer's Legal Survival Guide.* Multimedia Computing Corporation: Santa Clara, CA.

Index

DATE DUE

MAR 25 2013			
GAYLORD			PRINTED IN U.S.A.